Get started in German

German

Rosi McNab

For UK order enquiries: please contact Bookpoint Ltd, 130 Milton Park, Abingdon, Oxon OX14 4SB. *Telephone:* +44 (0) 1235 827720. *Fax:* +44 (0) 1235 400454. Lines are open 09.00–17.00, Monday to Saturday, with a 24-hour message answering service. Details about our titles and how to order are available at www.teachyourself.co.uk

For USA order enquiries: please contact McGraw-Hill Customer Services, PO Box 545, Blacklick, OH 43004-0545, USA. *Telephone:* 1-800-722-4726. *Fax:* 1-614-755-5645.

For Canada order enquiries: please contact McGraw-Hill Ryerson Ltd, 300 Water St, Whitby, Ontario L1N 9B6, Canada. *Telephone:* 905 430 5000. *Fax:* 905 430 5020.

Long renowned as the authoritative source for self-guided learning – with more than 50 million copies sold worldwide – the *teach yourself* series includes over 500 titles in the fields of languages, crafts, hobbies, business, computing and education.

British Library Cataloguing in Publication Data: a catalogue record for this title is available from the British Library.

Library of Congress Catalog Card Number: on file.

First published in UK 2012 by Hodder Education, part of Hachette Livre UK, 338 Euston Road, London, NW1 3BH.

First published in US 2012 by The McGraw-Hill Companies, Inc.

The *Teach Yourself* name is a registered trade mark of Hodder Headline.

Typeset by Integra Software Services Pvt. Ltd., Pondicherry, India.

Illustrated by Barking Dog Art, Sally Elford, Peter Lubach.

Printed in China for Hodder Education, an Hachette Livre UK Company, 338 Euston Road, London NW1 3BH

The publisher has used its best endeavours to ensure that the URLs for external websites referred to in this book are correct and active at the time of going to press. However, the publisher and the author have no responsibility for the websites and can make no guarantee that a site will remain live or that the content will remain relevant, decent or appropriate.

Hachette Livre UK's policy is to use papers that are natural, renewable and recyclable products and made from wood grown in sustainable forests. The logging and manufacturing processes are expected to conform to the environmental regulations of the country of origin.

Impression number	10 9 8 7 6
Year	2018

Contents

Personal introduction

Rosi McNab is an experienced language teacher and author. Her ground-breaking language training materials, books, videos, audio and interactive materials are in use in schools, colleges and homes all over the world.

She attributes her success to the fact that she always approaches language training from the learner's perspective, and she has spent most of her working life trying to create materials to help people of all abilities and from all walks of life to learn other languages. One of the biggest barriers to language learning is lack of confidence in one's own ability.

As a school pupil herself she was led to believe that she was 'no good' at languages, but later she found the difference between being taught and being helped to learn. For this reason, she is guided by what a learner can learn rather than what a book or teacher can teach. In books for beginners, she avoids complicated grammatical terminology and explains structures in layman's language and by example, and uses ways to help you learn by 'doing' rather than just reading.

The great Chinese philosopher Confucius said:

Read and forget

See and remember

Do and understand

This book is all about doing and understanding.

How the units work

Within each unit you will find the following components.

CONVERSATIONS

There are two conversations in each unit. The first one uses the polite form of 'you' and the second uses the familiar form so that you get plenty of practice with both forms. As you get more confident you should try covering up one side of the dialogue and see if you can still remember what to say. All the dialogues are also on the recording. You should practise saying them with the recording.

VOCABULARY

These contain key vocabulary and phrases which will help you to understand the text and build up a useful base for further study.   You should practise saying the words and expressions out loud after the tape. Try different ways to help you remember their meaning. Here are some ways you might find helpful:

▶ Cover up the English and see if you can remember what the words mean.
▶ Cover up the German and see if you can remember the German words.
▶ Write down the first letter of each word and see how many you can remember.
▶ Choose five new words or expressions and try to learn them.
▶ Try to relate them to English words which sound similar:

Gut – *good*, **danke** – *thanks*

THE DISCOVERY METHOD – LEARN TO LEARN!

There are lots of philosophies and approaches to language learning, some practical, some quite unconventional, and far too many to list here. Perhaps you know of a few, or even have some techniques of your own. In this book, we have incorporated the **Discovery method** of learning, a sort of DIY approach to language learning. What this means is that you will be encouraged throughout the course to engage your mind and figure out the language for yourself, through identifying patterns, understanding grammar concepts, noticing words that are similar to English, and more. This method promotes *language awareness*, a critical skill in acquiring a new language. As a result of your own efforts, you will be able to better retain what you have learned, use it with confidence, and, even better, apply those same skills to *continuing* to learn the language (or, indeed, another one) on your own after you've finished this book.

Everyone can succeed in learning a language – the key is to know *how to learn* it. Learning is more than just reading or memorizing grammar and vocabulary. It's about being an *active* learner, learning in real contexts, and, most importantly, *using* what you've learned in different situations. Simply put, if you **figure something out for yourself**, you're more likely to understand it. And when you use what you've learned, you're more likely to remember it.

And because many of the essential but (let's admit it!) dull details, such as grammar rules, are introduced through the **Discovery method**, you'll have more fun while learning. Soon, the language will start to make sense and you'll be relying on your own intuition to construct original sentences *independently*, not just listening and repeating.

Enjoy yourself!

EXERCISES

The various exercises provide practice in the German that you have learned in each unit.

The answers to the exercises are given at the back in the Answer key.

Listening exercises: You will need to use the recording for these.

 This symbol indicates that the recording is needed for the following section.

To make your learning easier and more efficient, a system of icons indicates the actions you should take:

 Listen and pronounce

 Figure something out for yourself

 Culture tip

 Exercises coming up!

 Speak German out loud

 Reading passage

 Writing task

 Check your German (no cheating)

Pronunciation guide

A few tips to help you acquire an authentic accent:

▶ Always say everything out loud, preferably as if you were talking to someone on the other side of the room!

▶ Listen carefully to the recording and use the gapped recordings to practice your pronunciation and fluency.

▶ Record your voice and compare it with the recording.

▶ Ask a native speaker to listen to your pronunciation and tell you how to improve it.

▶ Make a list of words that give you trouble and practise them.

And now practise saying these place names:

 00.01 **Pronunciation practice. Say these place names after the recording:**

Köln Bonn Berlin München Wien Zürich Düsseldorf Frankfurt Hamburg Hannover Leipzig Halle Freiburg Basel

[curl-n] [bon] [bairleen] [m*in-chen] [veen] [ts*irich] [d*isseldoorf] [frank-furt] [ham-burg] [hano-fer] [l-eye-pt-sich] [hal-uh] [fry-boorg] [bah-zel]

* **ü** sounds as if you were trying to say **u** but actually say **i**!

GERMAN SOUNDS

Most English speakers have little difficulty in pronouncing the German sounds because the two languages share some of their linguistic roots and they both belong to the same family of languages. Many German words are spoken out loud as they are spelt.

The consonants

 00.02

Most of these sounds are the same as in English. The ones which are not have asterisks:

b	as in *bath*	**Bad**
c	as in *camping*	**Campingplatz**
d	as in *dark*	**dunkel**
f	as in *free*	**frei**

g	as in *garden*	**Garten**
h	as in *hard*	**hart**
***j**	as y in *yes*	**ja**
k	as in *climb*	**klettern**
l	as in *last*	**letzte**
m	as in *man*	**Mann**
n	as in *night*	**Nacht**
p	as in *place*	**Platz**
***qu**	as *kv* in *Kvetch*	**Qualität** (*quality*)
r	produced at the back of the throat	**rot***
***s**	as *z* in *zone*	**Sohn** (*son*)
t	as in *tea*	**Tee**
***v**	as *f* in *follow*	**Volkswagen**
***w**	as *v* in *van*	**Wecker** (*alarm clock*)
x	as in *fax*	**Fax**
y	as *y* in *yen*	**Yen**
***z**	as *ts* in *tsetse*	**Zeitung** (*newspaper*)

The vowels

 00.03

The vowels have a long and short form.

The short form is normally used when followed by two or more consonants and the long form when followed by one consonant, or **h** + one consonant.

The short form is given first:

a as *a*	in *cat*	**Katze**
	father	**Vater**
e as *e*	in *bed*	**Bett**
ay	*day*	**Tee** (*tea*)
i as *i*	in *pit*	**mit** (*with*)
	kilo	**Kilo**
o as *o*	in *not*	**noch** (*yet*)
	home	**ohne** (*without*)

u as *u*	in *butcher*	**Bus**
	oe	in *shoe*	**Schuh**
			Guten Tag! (*good day*)

Special letters and sounds

 00.04

1   It is difficult to represent these sounds in English. If possible you should listen to the recording and practise them after it:

ä ö ü

¨ is called an '**Umlaut**' and is used on an **a, o** or **u**. It changes the sound of the word.

The short form is given first:

ä sounds	*eh*	**Mädchen** (*girl*)
	ay	**spät** (*late*)
ö sounds	*uh*	**wöchentlich** (*weekly*)
	er	**schön** (*pretty*)
ü sounds	*i*	**fünf** (*five*)
	u	**Bücher** (*books*), **Tür** (*door*)

2   **ß** represents '*ss*' and is used after a long vowel:
Straße (*street*), **Fuß** (*foot*)

3   **ch** is pronounced as *ch* in the Scottish word *loch*
ich (*I*) **Buch** (*book*)

4   **au** is pronounced *ow* as in *owl* **Frau** (*Mrs*)
 Auf Wiedersehen! (*goodbye*)
äu is pronounced *oy* as in *coy* **Fräulein** (*Miss*)

5   At the end of a word:

b	is pronounced *p*	**halb** (*half*)
d	is pronounced *t*	**Hund** (*dog*)
g	is pronounced *k*	**Tag** (*day*)
ig	is pronounced '*ch*	**fertig** (*ready*)

s	is pronounced *s* (not *z*)		**Haus** (*house*)	
e	is pronounced *-uh*:		**Bitte** (*please*)	
			Danke (*thanks*)	

| **6** **ei** is pronounced | *eye* | **dr**ei (*three*), | **W**ei**n** (*wine*) |
| **ie** is pronounced | *ee* | **v**ie**r** (*four*), | **B**ie**r** (*beer*) |

7 **sch** is pronounced	*sh* as in	**Sch**uh (*shoe*)
sp is pronounced	*shp* as in	**sp**ät (*late*)
st is pronounced	*sht* as in	**St**adt (*town*)

Pronunciation guide

Use this page to keep a list of words that are difficult to pronounce. Practise them often until you feel confident.

Guten Tag!
Hello!

In this unit, you will learn how to:
▶ *say 'hello' and 'goodbye'.*
▶ *give your name.*
▶ *use common greetings.*
▶ *say where you are from.*
▶ *learn about the formal and informal words for 'you'.*

CEFR: (A1) *Can establish basic social contact by using the simplest everyday polite forms of: greetings and farewells; introductions; etc.*

Visiting Germany

Deutschland *(Germany)* with 81 million inhabitants is the largest economy in the **Europäische Union** *(EU – European Union)*. **Die deutsche Sprache** *(the German language)* is spoken by about 105 million native speakers and another 80 million speakers world wide in countries like **die Schweiz** *(Switzerland)*, **Österreich** *(Austria)* and **Namibien** *(Namibia)*.

Berlin is the capital city. **Hamburg**, situated on the river **Elbe** in **Norddeutschland** *(North Germany)*, is the second largest city and third biggest port in Europe despite being 110 km from the sea. **München** *(Munich)* in **Bayern** *(Bavaria)* in **Süddeutschland** *(South Germany)* is the third biggest city and the home of BMW. The fourth largest city is the important economic and cultural centre **Köln** *(Cologne)* situated on the river **Rhein** *(Rhine)* and **Frankfurt am Main** is the home of the **Europäische Zentralbank** *(EZB – the European Central Bank)*.

Look at the words in bold above. Can you work out how to say north, south and European in German?

Vocabulary builder

 01.01 **Look at the words and phrases and complete the missing English expressions.**

 Then listen to these words and see if any sound like English words you know.

Cover up the English and see if you can remember what they mean.

GREETINGS

Guten Tag	*Good day*
Guten Abend	*Good evening*
Guten Morgen	*Good* _____
Gute Nacht	*Good* _____
Hallo	*Hello*
Auf Wiedersehen	*Goodbye*
Tschüs *or* **Tschüss**	*Bye*

> **AS A GENERAL RULE YOU USE:**
> **Guten Morgen** first thing in the morning,
> **Guten Tag** after about 10 a.m.,
> **Guten Abend** after 5 p.m.,
> **Gute Nacht** when you are going to bed.
> In South Germany and Austria people often say:
> **Grüß Gott!** (lit. *greet God*) which means *Good day!*

NEW EXPRESSIONS

Wie heißen Sie?	*What's your name?*
Ich heiße...	*I'm called...*
Angenehm.	*Pleased to meet you.*
Wie geht's?	*How are you?*
Gut danke, und Ihnen?	*Well thanks, and you?*
Ich verstehe nicht.	*I don't understand.*
Sprechen Sie Englisch?	*Do you speak English?*
Trinken Sie einen Kaffee?	*Do you want a coffee?*
Nein, danke.	*No, thank you.*
Ja, bitte.	*Yes, please.*

> **ß** represents **ss** and is used after a long vowel: **Straße** (*street*), **Fuß** (*foot*).

Conversation

 01.02 *John Brown has just arrived in Germany and is meeting Herr Schuhmacher for the first time. Listen and follow the text. Then answer the question.*

1 What time of day do you think it is? _____

Herr Schuhmacher	Guten Tag.
John	Guten Tag.
Herr Schuhmacher	Wie heißen Sie?
John	Ich verstehe nicht.
Herr Schuhmacher	Mein Name ist Schuhmacher, Udo Schuhmacher.
	Wie heißen Sie?
John	Ich heiße John Brown.
Herr Schuhmacher	Angenehm. Wie geht's?
John	Gut danke, und Ihnen?
Herr Schuhmacher	Gut danke ... Trinken Sie einen Kaffee?
John	Ich verstehe nicht. Sprechen Sie Englisch?
Herr Schuhmacher	Nein, leider nicht. Kaffee? ähm ... coffee?
John	Ja ... bitte ...
Herr Schuhmacher	Zucker ... sugar?
John	Nein, danke.
Herr Schuhmacher	Ja also, bis morgen. Auf Wiedersehen.
John	Auf Wiedersehen.

In normal conversation when answering the question *What's your name?* you wouldn't need to say *I am called* (**Ich heiße...**) or *my name is* (**Mein Name ist...**), but here we practise the full reply to help you to get used to the pattern of the language.

01.03 Listen again and speak John's part.

2 Match the questions and answers.

   a Wie heißen Sie?   **i** Auf Wiedersehen.
   b Wie geht es Ihnen?   **ii** Guten Tag.
   c Auf Wiedersehen.   **iii** Ich heiße John.
   d Sprechen Sie Englisch?   **iv** Nein, danke.
   e Trinken Sie einen Kaffee? **v** Gut danke, und Ihnen?
   f Guten Tag.   **vi** Leider nicht.

3 **What do you think? Read the conversation and answer the questions below.**

  a Are Herr Schuhmacher and John old friends?
  b What is Herr Schuhmacher's first name?
  c How is John?
  d How is Herr Schuhmacher?
  e John asks Herr Schuhmacher if he speaks English. He replies, **Nein, leider nicht**. Does he speak English or not? What do you think it means?

Language discovery

1 **Find the expressions in the conversation that mean:**

  a Do you speak English?
  b Good day.
  c I don't understand.
  d Goodbye.
  e Pleased to meet you.
  f How are you?

Now cover up your answers and see if you can say them without looking at the conversation.

2 **Which words from the conversation mean the same as the expressions below? Which word do you think is used for *you*?**

  a What's your name?
  b Do you want a coffee?

Learn more

In German there are two ways of addressing people: a formal way and an informal way. You use the formal way when addressing:

▶ someone you don't know
▶ someone who is older than you
▶ someone to whom you want to show respect.

The key word to listen for is Sie followed by verbs ending with -en, such as: heißen (*to be called*), **trinken** (*to drink*), **gehen** (*to go*), **verstehen** (*to understand*), or **sprechen** (*to speak*).

> Remember! In German, the verb endings change to 'agree' with the subject of the verb.
> Ich (*I*)   Ich gehe.
> Sie (*you*)   Sie gehen.

In English, we often start a question with *Do* as in *Do you speak English? Do you understand?* German (and most other European languages) don't use *do*, they just start with the verb: *Speak you English? Understand you? Drink you a coffee?* It may sound abrupt but it is quite normal. Try it: **Sprechen Sie Englisch? Verstehen Sie? Trinken Sie einen Kaffee?**

Capital letters keep popping up where you don't expect them. This is because in German all nouns begin with a capital letter. Not sure what a noun is? A noun is a naming word. You can use *the*, *a* or *my* in front of it.

das Buch – *the book*   **ein Auto** – *a car*   **mein Freund** – *my friend*

Gut becomes **Guten** in front of **Morgen, Tag** and **Abend**, but **Gut** becomes **Gute** in front of **Nacht**. Want to know why? All will be explained later! For now, say them out loud to help you remember them.

 PRACTICE

1 What verb endings appear with *Sie*? Complete the verbs.
   a Wie heiß _____ Sie?
   b Trink _____ Sie einen Kaffee?
   c Sprech _____ Sie Englisch?
   d Versteh _____ Sie Deutsch?
   e Geh _____ Sie ins Restaurant?
   f Wohn _____ Sie in London?

2 What verb ending appears after *Ich*? Complete the verbs.
   a Ich heiß _____ Klaus.
   b Ich versteh _____ nicht.

3 What are the nouns in these German sentences?
   a Trinken Sie einen Kaffee? *Would you like a coffee?*
   b Ich gehe in ein Restaurant. *I'm going to a restaurant.*
   c Hier ist mein Buch. *Here's my book.*
   d Das Auto ist neu. *The car is new.*
   e Mein Freund hat ein neues Auto. *My friend has a new car.*

 Listen and learn

1 01.04 **Listen to the conversation. What are these people saying? Write the correct number.**

| **i** *Good morning* | **ii** *Good day* | **iii** *Good evening* | **iv** *Good night* |

a _____   **c** _____

b _____   **d** _____

2 01.05 **Who is speaking to whom? Match the speakers.**

a Herr Braun   **i** Jane
b Uta   **ii** Frau Müller
c Herr Fischer   **iii** Knut
d Jens   **iv** Brigitte

3 01.06 **Listen and fill in the missing word.**

a Guten _____, Herr Fischer.
b Wie heißen _____?
c Mein _____ ist Braun, Heinrich Braun.
d _____ geht es Ihnen?
e _____ Sie Englisch?
f Gut _____ und Ihnen?
g _____ Sie einen Kaffee?
h _____ verstehe nicht.
i Nein, _____.

> In German, you pronounce every letter, so try to copy the pronunciation you hear on the recording.

 4 01.07 **Now listen and say these phrases out loud.**

▶ Auf Wiedersehen.
▶ Ich verstehe nicht.
▶ Wie geht es Ihnen?
▶ Wie heißen Sie?

Conversation

01.08 *Listen and follow the text. Then answer the questions.*

1 Where does Thorsten come from? Where does Jane come from?

Thorsten	Hallo, ich heiße Thorsten. Wie heißt du?
Jane	Jane.
Thorsten	Wie geht's Jane?
Jane	Gut danke und dir?
Thorsten	Auch gut, danke. Woher kommst du?
Jane	Aus England.
Thorsten	Wo wohnst du? In London?
Jane	Nein ich wohne in Manchester, in Nordengland. Woher kommst du?
Thorsten	Ich? Aus Süddeutschland.
Jane	Wo wohnst du?
Thorsten	In München. Trinkst du einen Kaffee?
Jane	Ja gerne.
Thorsten	Gut, gehen wir in die Bar.
Später (Later) …	
Jane	Danke für den Kaffee.
Thorsten	Nichts zu danken. Tschüs.
Jane	Tschüs.

01.09 **Listen again to the conversation.**

2 Review the expressions below from the conversation. Then match them to the English meaning.

a Woher kommst du?
b Aus England.
c Wo wohnst du?
d Gerne.
e Nichts zu danken.
f Tschüs.

i *Gladly/Willingly.*
ii *Where are you from?*
iii *Bye.*
iv *Don't mention it.*
v *Where do you live?*
vi *From England.*

 Language discovery

Which words from the conversation mean the same as the expressions below? Which word do you think is being used for *you* this time?

1 What's your name?

2 Where do you live?

Learn more

You have already learned the formal way of addressing people. Now let's look at the informal. You use the informal way when:

▶ talking to a friend

▶ you use first names

▶ you speak to a younger person.

The key word to listen for is **du** followed by verbs ending with **-st**, such as **heißt** *(to be called)*, **trinkst** *(to drink)*, **gehst** *(to go)*, **verstehst** *(to understand)*, or **sprechst** *(to speak)*.

> **SPEAKING TIP**
> You only need to use *du* or *Sie* when asking a question, so listen to find out which form they use when speaking to you and use the same form in return!

 PRACTICE

1 What verb endings appear with *du*? Complete the verbs.

a Wo wohn_____ du?

b Woher komm_____ du?

c Trink_____ du einen Kaffee?

2 *Sie* or *du*? Which form is being used?

a Wo wohnen _____?

b Woher kommst _____?

c Trinken _____ einen Kaffee?

d Sprechen _____ Englisch?

e Verstehst_____?

f Trinkst _____ einen Kaffee?

 3 01.10 **Which form of *you* is being used?**

a du   Sie

b du   Sie

c du   Sie

d du   Sie

e du   Sie

f du   Sie

4 Choose the right word to complete the sentences.

   a Woher (kommst/kommen) Sie?

   b (Sprichst/Sprechen) Sie Englisch?

   c Woher (kommst/kommen) du?

   d (Trinkst/trinken) Sie einen Kaffee?

 5 Now prepare and give your own answers to these questions.

   a Wie heißt du?

   b Wie geht's?

> You might want to say:
> **Ich komme aus...**

   c Woher kommst du?

Schottland	*Scotland*
Irland	*Ireland*
Wales	*Wales*
Amerika	*America*
den Vereinigten Staaten	*the USA*

Reading and writing

 1 Read the email. Can you figure out the meaning of the following words?

   a Ich lerne _____ .

   b Lernst du _____ ?

Ich heiße Thorsten. Ich wohne in München in Süddeutschland. Ich lerne Englisch. Was lernst du?

Tschüs

2 Answer the questions.

   a What is the writer's name?

   b Where does he live?

   c What is he learning?

 3 Now write a response using what Thorsten has written as a model.

Test yourself

1 01.11 **Listen to these people and choose the correct time of day.**

a	early morning	later in the morning	late afternoon	night time
b	early morning	later in the morning	late afternoon	night time
c	early morning	later in the morning	late afternoon	night time
d	early morning	later in the morning	late afternoon	night time

2 01.12 **Which form of talking are these people using?**

- **a** formal ☐ informal ☐
- **b** formal ☐ informal ☐
- **c** formal ☐ informal ☐
- **d** formal ☐ informal ☐
- **e** formal ☐ informal ☐

3 Choose the right words from the box to complete the sentences.

> komme   kommst   kommen   sprechen
> sprichst   wohne   wohnst   wohnen

- **a** Woher _____ Sie?
- **b** Ich _____ aus England
- **c** _____ Sie in London?
- **d** Ich _____ in Manchester.
- **e** _____ Sie Deutsch?
- **f** Woher _____ du?
- **g** _____ du in Deutschland?
- **h** _____ du Englisch?

SELF CHECK

	I CAN. . .
◯	. . . say *hello* and *goodbye*
◯	. . . ask how someone is
◯	. . . say how I am
◯	. . . give my name
◯	. . . say *I don't understand*
◯	. . . ask someone if they speak English
◯	. . . ask someone where they are from
◯	. . . say where I come from

2 Kaffee und Kuchen
Coffee and cakes

In this unit, you will learn how to:
▶ *say what you like to drink.*
▶ *say 'please' and 'thank you'.*
▶ *ask to have something repeated.*
▶ *build new words.*
▶ *express likes and preferences.*
▶ *recognize and use the numbers from 1 to 20.*

CEFR: (A2) *Can establish basic social contact by saying please, thank you, sorry, etc. and can interact in a simple way provided the other person talks slowly and clearly and is prepared to help.*

 Kaffeepause

Kaffee und Kuchen is a German tradition, the equivalent of the British afternoon tea. You may well be invited to have **eine Tasse Kaffee** (*a cup of coffee*) at any time of the day, or you may be invited to have **Kaffee und Kuchen** in the **Nachmittag** (*afternoon*) or at the **Wochenende** (*weekend*).

You will usually be offered quite strong **Filterkaffee** in preference to **Pulverkaffee** (*instant powder coffee*) served with **kalter Milch** (*cold milk*) or **Kaffeesahne** (*cream for coffee – similar to evaporated milk*) and **Zucker** (*white sugar*) or **Kandis** (*crystallized sugar lumps*).

You might prefer your **Kaffee koffeinfrei** or **entkoffeiniert** and if you want it sweet but without sugar you ask for **Süßstoff**.

Of course in most places you can also ask for a **Cappuccino**, **Espresso** or even a **Latte** as the Italian names are used internationally, but they might not always be available as many people prefer their own style of coffee.

 Look at the words in bold above. Can you figure out how to say *decaffeinated coffee* **and** *sweetener*? **Can you find four words which look or sound like English words?**

Vocabulary builder

ORDERING FOOD AND BEVERAGES

02.01 Look at the words and phrases and complete the missing English expressions. Then listen to these words and see if any sound like English words you know. Cover up the English and see if you can remember what they mean.

GETRÄNKE DRINKS

eine Tasse Kaffee	*a cup of coffee*
eine Tasse Tee	*a _____ of _____*
eine Tasse heisse Schokolade	*a cup of hot _____*
ein Kännchen Kaffee	*a pot of coffee*
ein Glas Mineralwasser	*a glass of mineral water*
ein Glas Wein	*a _____ of wine*
eine Flasche Rotwein/Weisswein	*a bottle of red wine/ white wine*
ein Bier	*a beer*
eine Dose Cola	*a can of coca cola*
einen Orangensaft	*an orange juice*
ein Stück Kuchen	*a piece of cake*
mit/ohne...	*with /without*
Sahne	*cream*
Milch	*milk*
Zitrone	*lemon*
Zucker	*sugar*

NEW EXPRESSIONS

Look at the expressions that are used in the next dialogue. Note their meanings.

Möchten Sie...?	*Would you like...?*
Ich möchte...	*I would like...*
Haben Sie (Süßstoff)?	*Have you got (sweetener)...?*

> **PRONUNCIATION TIPS**
> **z** at the beginning of a word sounds like *ts*
> **ß** is a double *ss*
> **w** is pronounced *v*
> **v** is pronounced *f*
> **ie** sounds *ee*
> **ei** sounds *aye*
> **sch** sounds soft as in <u>sh</u>ut
> **Stück** sounds a bit like <u>shtook</u>

> **THE UMLAUT**
> The two dots on the **ö** is called an **Umlaut** and 'squashes' the sound of the **o**, so **Ich möchte** sounds a bit like **ich murckte**. The umlaut can also be used on **a** as in **Getränke** and **u** as in **Stück**, but listen to the recording to hear it properly.

Conversation

 02.02 *John is visiting Frau Fischer. Listen and follow the text. Then answer the question.*

1 What does Frau Fischer offer John to drink and eat?

Frau Fischer	Guten Tag, wie gehts?
John	Gut danke, und Ihnen?
Frau Fischer	Gut ... Trinken Sie eine Tasse Kaffee?
John	Ja, bitte.
Frau Fischer	Mit Milch und Zucker?
John	Ohne Milch, schwarz bitte. Haben Sie Süßstoff?
Frau Fischer	Bitte schön. ... Geht das so?
John	Ja ... gut!
Frau Fischer	Möchten Sie ein Stück Kuchen?
John	Wie bitte? Ich verstehe nicht.
Frau Fischer	Ein Stück Kuchen? Schokoladenkuchen?
John	Ja, gerne!
Frau Fischer	Mit Sahne?
John	Nein danke, ohne Sahne.
Frau Fischer	Bitte schön.
John	Danke.
Frau Fischer	Bitte, bitte.

2.03 **Listen again and speak John's part.**

2 Match the questions and answers.

a Trinken Sie eine Tasse Kaffee?   i Bitte schön.
b Mit Milch und Zucker?   ii Ohne Sahne.
c Haben sie Süßstoff?   iii Ja, bitte.
d Möchten Sie ein Stück Kuchen?   iv Ohne Milch.
e Mit Sahne?   v Ja, gerne.

3 What do you think? Read the conversation again and answer the questions below.

a How does John want his coffee?
b What else does he ask for?
c What does she offer him to have with his coffee?
d Does he want some?
e What does he not want?

 Language discovery

1 Find the German expressions in the conversation.

   a Would you like a piece of cake?

   b Yes, please.

   c Yes, please!

   d I don't understand.

   e No thanks.

   f Is it OK?

   g Without cream.

   h With milk.

Now cover up your answers and see if you can say them without looking at the conversation.

2 Which words from the conversation mean the same as the expressions below?

   a Have you got...?

   b Would you like...?

Learn more

You will notice that **bitte** appears frequently in the dialogue. It is a very useful word. It can mean:

Bitte	*Please* or *Yes, please.*
Wie bitte?	*Pardon?*
Bitte schön.	*Here you are.* (When handing something to someone.)
Bitte!	*Sorry!* as in *'I didn't mean to bump into you.'*
Bitte, bitte!	*Don't mention it.* (When someone says thank you.)

Did you notice? In German, you don't use the word *of*. You just say *a glass wine, a bottle beer.*

A lot of German words look very long. Many German words are actually two or even three words joined together to make one long word. Find the place where these joined-up words divide and work out what the different parts mean. For example:

Schokoladenkuchen = **Schokolade** + **Kuchen** = *chocolate cake*

Schwarzwälderkirschtorte = **Schwarzwald** *(Black Forest)* + **Kirsch** *(cherry)* + **Torte** *(gateau)* = *Black Forest gâteau (a chocolate cake decorated with sour cherries and cream)*

1 Which bitte is it? Match the words with their definitions.

a	Bitte	**i**	*Don't mention it*
b	Wie bitte?	**ii**	*Here you are*
c	Bitte schön	**iii**	*Sorry!*
d	Bitte!	**iv**	*Pardon?*
e	Bitte, bitte!	**v**	*Please*

2 Using the words you have learnt and Apfel *(apple)* and Käse *(cheese)*, give the German for the following words.

a apple cake
b cheese cake
c cream gateau
d mineral water
e red wine

Learn more

 02.04 **DIE ZAHLEN VON 1 BIS 20** *THE NUMBERS FROM 1 TO 20*

0	**null**	5	**fünf** *(finf)*	10	**zehn** *(tsayn)*
1	**eins** *((h)eins)*	6	**sechs** *(zex)*	11	**elf**
2	**zwei** *(tsv-eye)*	7	**sieben** *(zeebun)*	12	**zwölf** *(tsvulf)*
3	**drei** *(dry)*	8	**acht** *(akht)*		
4	**vier** *(fear)*	9	**neun** *(noyn)*		

German numbers are easy to learn. If you learn the numbers 1–12, you will be able to say all the numbers up to 20. For the 'teens' just add *three, four* etc. to *ten*. Look at the following:

Thirteen is '*three+ten*'	**dreizehn**	
Fourteen is '*four+ten*'	**vierzehn**	
Fifteen is '*five+ten*'	**fünfzehn**	
For *sixteen*, **sechs** loses its last '*s*'	**sechzehn**	
For *seventeen*, **sieben** loses its '**en**'	**siebzehn**	
Eighteen is '*eight+ten*'	**achtzehn**	
Nineteen is '*nine+ten*'	**neunzehn**	
Twenty is	**zwanzig**	

> **TO LEARN NUMBERS**
> ► Read all the numbers out loud or listen to the recording and copy saying the numbers.
> ► Try to say the first six numbers without looking. Now try the numbers six to 12.
> ► Now say the numbers 13–20 and say them out loud. Remember that 16 and 17 need special treatment.

PRACTICE 2

1 What are these numbers? Say them out loud.

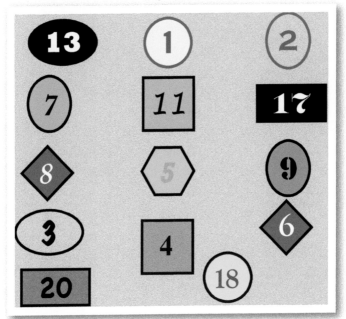

2 02.05 **Now listen and write down the numbers as numerals.**

a 7   b __   c __   d __   e __

f __   g __   h __   i __   j __

k __   l __   m __   n __   o __

p __   q __   r __   s __   t __

3 02.05 **Now listen and practise saying the numbers out loud.**

Listen and learn

1 02.06 **Listen and say these words out loud.**

a Zucker Zitrone

b ein Wein

c Wie viel

d vier Bier

e Kännchen Getränke

f Süßstoff Stück Tschüs

2 02.07 **What are these people being offered? Listen and write the letter of the speaker next to the correct picture.**

1 Milch _____

2 _____

3 _____

4 _____

5 _____

6 _____

7 _____

8 _____

9 _____

3 Now ask for the same things yourself. Start with: Ich möchte ... .

4 02.08 **How many are they ordering? Listen and write down the missing number.**

a _____ Gläser Bier.
b _____ Tassen Kaffee.
c _____ Tassen Schokolade mit Sahne.

d _____ Stück Kuchen.
e _____ Orangensaft.
f _____ Dosen Cola.

Conversation

 02.09 Jane and Thorsten are in the hotel bar. Listen and read the text. Then answer the question.

1 What drinks do they order?

Thorsten	Trinkst du ein Glas Wein?
Jane	Gerne!
Thorsten	Trinkst du lieber Rotwein oder Weißwein?
Jane	Weißwein.
Thorsten	Süß oder trocken?
Jane	Wie bitte? Ich verstehe nicht.
Thorsten	Süß oder trocken?
Jane	ah ... Halbtrocken.
Thorsten	Möchtest du ein Glas Prosecco?
Jane	Was ist das?
Thorsten	Italienischer Champagner.
Jane	Perfekt! Ich trinke gern Champagner.
Kellner (*waiter*)	Was darf es sein?
Thorsten	Ein Bier und ein Glas Prosecco.
Kellner	Ein Pils und ein Prosecco, bitte schön!
Thorsten	Danke schön. Zum Wohl!
Jane	Zum Wohl!
Thorsten	Schmeckt's?
Jane	Ja, genau richtig!
Thorsten	Gut ... also was machst du hier in Berlin? ...

02.10 **Listen again and speak Jane's part.**

2 Review the expressions below from the conversation. Then match them to the English meanings.

a Trinkst du lieber Rotwein oder Weißwein?
b Süß oder trocken?
c Halbtrocken.
d Möchtest du ein Glas Prosecco?
e Zum Wohl!

i *Cheers!*
ii *Medium dry*
iii *Would you like a glass of Prosecco?*
iv *Would you like red or white wine?*
v *Sweet or dry?*

3 Can you figure out how to say the following?

   a How does it taste?

   b Just right!

Learn more

GERN UND LIEBER *LIKING AND PREFERRING*

Instead of using the verbs *to like* and *to prefer*, the words **gern** or **lieber** are used after the verb in German.

gern – *you do it willingly/with pleasure*   **lieber** – *you prefer it*

Ich trinke gern Weißwein   *I like (drinking) white wine*

   aber ich trinke lieber Rotwein.   *but I prefer (drinking) red wine.*

QUESTIONS

Sie form	Du form	
Essen Sie gern...?	**Isst du gern...?**	*Do you like (to eat...)?*
Essen Sie lieber...?	**Isst du lieber...?**	*Do you prefer (to eat...)?*
Trinken Sie gern...?	**Trinkst du gern?**	*Do you like (to drink...)?*
Trinken Sie lieber...?	**Trinkst du lieber?**	*Do you prefer (to drink...)?*

REPLIES

Ich esse gern...	*I like (to eat...)*
Ich esse lieber...	*I prefer (I would rather eat...)*
Ich trinke gern...	*I like (to drink...)*
Ich trinke lieber...	*I prefer (I would rather drink...)*

When you use **gern** and **lieber** you have to say what it is that you like doing.

PRACTICE 3

1 Match the questions to the answers.

   a Essen Sie gern Chinesisch?

   b Trinken Sie gern Bier?

   c Spielen Sie gern Tennis?

   d Tanzen Sie gern Zumba?

   i Ich tanze nicht gern.

   ii Ich spiele Tennis nicht gern. Ich spiele lieber Squash.

   iii Ich trinke gern Bier, aber ich trinke lieber Wein.

   iv Ich esse gern Chinesisch, aber ich esse lieber Curry.

2 02.11 **Listen to find out what they prefer. Choose the correct answer.**

a	**i**	Rotwein	**ii**	Weißwein
b	**i**	Tee	**ii**	Kaffee
c	**i**	Bier	**ii**	Mineralwasser
d	**i**	Tee mit Milch	**ii**	Tee mit Zitrone
e	**i**	Kaffee mit Milch	**ii**	Kaffee ohne Milch
f	**i**	Kuchen mit Sahne	**ii**	Kuchen ohne Sahne
g	**i**	Pizza	**ii**	Spaghetti

3 Now prepare and give your own responses to these questions.

   a Trinkst du gern Bier?
   b Trinkst du lieber Rotwein oder Weißwein?
   c Süß oder trocken?
   d Möchtest du ein Glas Prosecco?
   e Zum Wohl!
   f Schmeckt's?

4 02.12 **Listen to find out how much the items on the menu cost.**

Heiße Getränke

Tasse Kaffee	€ _____
Becher Kaffee	€ _____
Tasse Schokolade	€ _____
Becher Schokolade mit Sahne	€ _____
Tasse schwarzer Tee	€ _____
Glas Kamillentee	€ _____
Glas Pfefferminztee	€ _____
Glas grüner Tee	€ _____
Orangensaft	€ _____
Apfelsaft	€ _____

5 Can you figure out which is bigger – a Becher or a Tasse? _____

6 Now order drinks for yourself and your friends from the menu.
   Ich möchte _____ für mich
   und _____ für meinen Freund
   und _____ für meine Freundin.

7 02.13 **What do these people order?**

a _____		**b** _____		**c** _____	
d _____		**e** _____		**f** _____	

Reading and writing

1 Read the paragraph below. Then answer the questions.

Ich stehe um sieben Uhr auf und trinke einen Orangensaft.
Im Büro trinke ich einen Kaffee, schwarz, ohne Zucker, und
zu Mittag trinke ich Mineralwasser. Nachmittags trinke ich
nochmal Kaffee aber dann trinke ich lieber entkoffeinierten
Kaffee mit Kandis. Abends trinke ich ein Glas Weißwein.
Ich trinke lieber Weißwein als Rotwein. Bier und Cola
schmecken mir nicht. Was trinkst du?

Birgit

    a What does Birgit drink when she gets up?
    b What does she drink in the office?
    c What does she drink at lunch time?
    d What does she drink in the afternoon?
    e What does she drink in the evening?
    f What does she not like to drink?

2 Write a paragraph saying what you like and don't like to drink using Birgit's writing as a model.

 Test yourself

1 Look at the pictures. What would you ask for?

    a _____

    b _____

c _____

d _____

e _____

f _____

2 Look at the drinks on the table.

a What would you say to order them? Say your order out loud and start with: **Ich möchte** ... .

b Now write a list of what has been ordered.

3 Was machen Sie?

What do you do?

In this unit, you will learn how to:
▶ *say what you do and ask someone what they do.*
▶ *say where you work and ask someone where they work.*
▶ *say and recognize the days of the week.*
▶ *say and recognize the months of the year.*
▶ *say when your birthday is.*
▶ *say what your phone number is.*
▶ *say the numbers 20–100.*
▶ *tell the time using the 24-hour clock.*

CEFR: (A2) *Can communicate in simple and routine tasks requiring a simple and direct exchange of information on familiar and routine matters to do with work and personal information.*

Der Arbeitstag *The working day*

Germans have a reputation for hard work and **Herr Schuhmacher** is no exception. He is a **Finanzberater** *(financial advisor)* and works **in einer Bank** *(in a bank)*. When he is in the office, his working day usually begins **um acht Uhr** *(at 8 a.m.)* and finishes **um 18.00 Uhr** *(at 6 p.m.)*. His wife is a **Krankenpflegerin** *(nurse)* and she works **in einem Krankenhaus** *(in a hospital)*. She works **Halbzeit** *(half-time)*. Her **Arbeitstag** *(working day)* usually begins **um halb neun** *(at 8.30 a.m.)* and she finishes **um halb eins** *(12.30)* but she sometimes also has to work **Samstag vormittag** *(Saturday morning)*.

Look at the words in bold above. How do they say:
  1 at eight o'clock   **3** at 6 p.m.
  2 at 8.30   **4** at 12.30

What did you notice about the last two? In German, instead of saying *half past twelve* they say halb _____ and instead of saying *a.m.* and *p.m.* they use the _____ hour clock.

Vocabulary builder

03.01 Look at these words and phrases and complete the missing English expressions. Then listen to these words and see if any sound like English words. Cover up the English and see if you can remember what they mean.

JOBS

der Beruf	*job /employment*
Was sind Sie von Beruf?	*What (job) do you do?*
Ich bin Verkaufsleiter/Verkaufsleiterin.	*I am a sales representative.*

Most job titles have a masculine and feminine form:

Schauspieler (m)	*actor*
Schauspielerin (f)	*actress*

The feminine form is usually made by adding -*in* to the masculine:

Geschäftsführer/Geschäftsführerin	*manager*
Lehrer/Lehrerin	*teacher*
Reiseleiter/Reiseleiterin	*travel guide*
Arzt/Ärztin	*doctor*

03.01 What do you think these words mean?

Polizist/Polizistin _____

Journalist/Journalistin _____

Student/Studentin _____

NEW EXPRESSIONS

Sind Sie berufstätig?	*Do you work?*
Ich bin persönlicher Assistent.	*I'm a personal assistant.*
Was macht Ihr Mann?	*What does your husband do?*
Er ist Unternehmensberater.	*He's a business consultant.*
Was macht Ihre Frau?	*What does your wife do?*
Sie ist Krankenpflegerin.	*She's a nurse.*
Sie arbeitet in einem Krankenhaus.	*She works in a hospital.*

Conversation

 Herr Schuhmacher and John are in the hotel bar. Listen and follow the text. Then answer the question.

1 What are they talking about?

  a their hometown b their jobs c their local hospital

Herr Schuhmacher	Sind Sie berufstätig?
John	Wie bitte?
Herr Schuhmacher	Was sind Sie von Beruf?
John	Ich bin Manager.
Herr Schuhmacher	Wo arbeiten Sie?
John	ähm ... In der Freizeitindustrie.
Herr Schuhmacher	Was machen Sie hier in Deutschland?
John	Ich mache einen Sprachkursus. Ich lerne Deutsch.
	Was machen Sie?
Herr Schuhmacher	Ich bin Finanzberater. Ich arbeite in einer Bank.
	Sind Sie verheiratet?
John	Nein. Ich habe eine Freundin.
Herr Schuhmacher	Was macht sie?
John	Sie ist Krankenpflegerin. Sie arbeitet in einem Krankenhaus.
Herr Schuhmacher	Meine Frau ist Physiotherapeutin. Sie arbeitet in einer Klinik.
	Wo arbeiten Sie?
John	In einem Büro in London. Und Sie?
Herr Schuhmacher	Ich? Bei einer Bank in Frankfurt ... aber ich reise viel.
John	Ich auch!

03.03 **Listen and speak John's part.**

2 Match the questions and answers.
  a Was sind Sie von Beruf?   **i** Sie arbeitet in einem Krankenhaus.
  b Wo arbeiten Sie?   **ii** Sie ist Krankenpflegerin.
  c Sind Sie verheiratet?   **iii** Ich arbeite in der Freizeitindustrie.
  d Was macht sie?   **iv** Ich bin Manager.
  e Wo arbeitet sie?   **v** Nein. Ich habe eine Freundin.

3 **What do you think? Read the conversation and say which statements are true (T) and which are false (F).**

   a John works as a sales representative.
   b He is doing a German course.
   c He isn't married.
   d Herr Schuhmacher works in a hospital.

 # Language discovery

1 **Find the expressions in the conversation.**

   a leisure industry
   b financial advisor
   c a language course
   d are you married?

2 **Find these words or parts of words in the conversation. Write the English word next to them.**

   a hier _____
   b Finanz _____
   c haus _____
   d Klinik _____

> **DID YOU NOTICE?**
> The words for *you* (**Sie**) and *she* (**sie**) look and sound the same – how do you know which one is being used?
> After **Sie** *(you)* the verb ends in **-en**; after **sie** *(she)* and **er** *(he)* the verb ends in **-t.**

3 **Find the expressions in the conversation.**

   a What do you do?
   b What does she do?

4 ***You* or *she*? Choose the correct word.**

   a Wo arbeiten Sie?
   b Sie arbeiten in der Ölindustrie.
   c Sie arbeitet im Finanzwesen.
   d Wo arbeitet sie?

arbeiten – *to work*	
Singular	**Plural**
ich arbeite – *I work*	**wir arbeiten** – *we work*
du (familiar) **arbeitest** – *you work*	**Ihr** (familiar) **arbeitet** – *you work*
er/sie arbeitet – *he/she works*	**sie arbeiten** – *they work*
Sie (polite form for *you*, singular and plural) **arbeiten** – *you work*	

Learn more

When you say what job you do, you do not use the article *a* as you do in English. In German, *I am a student* is **Ich bin Student.**

1 Look at the conversation to see what the missing words should be.

a *in an office*   in einem _____
b *in a hospital*   in einem _____
c *in a clinic*   in einer _____
d *in a bank*   in einer _____

Why are there two forms? Because in German all nouns are masculine, feminine or neuter and the words for *a* **(ein, eine)** and *the* **(der, die, das)** sometimes change after *in*! Complicated? Just learn the phrases you need and if you get them wrong you will still be understood!

masculine/neuter	feminine	
in einem Salon *in a salon*	**in einer Fabrik**	*in a factory*
in einem Restaurant *in a restaurant*	**in einer Firma**	*in a business*
in einem Schuhgeschäft *in a shoe shop*	**in einer Schule**	*in a school*

* If you want to say what industry you work in, use **in der Freizeitindustrie** as a pattern **(in der Textilindustrie, in der Ölindustrie, in der Automobilindustrie).**

2 Choose the correct answer.

a Where would you expect a **Krankenpfleger** to work?

i **in einem Reisebüro** ii **in einem Friseursalon**
iii **in einem Krankenhaus**

b Where would you expect a **Bankangestellte** to work?

i **in einer Bank** ii **in einem Supermarkt** iii **in einem Restaurant**

c Where would you expect a **Lehrer** to work?

i **in einer Klinik** ii **in einem Geschäft** iii **in einer Schule**

 Listen and learn

1 03.04 **What do they do? Listen and write the correct letter. Use the professions in the box.**

> 1 hairdresser 2 nurse 3 secretary 4 teacher
> 5 physiotherapist 6 salesperson

2 03.05 **Wo arbeiten sie?** *Where do they work?* **Listen and write the correct letter. Use the work places in the box. You don't have to understand every word to get the answer. Just listen for clues!**

> 1 bank 2 garage 3 hospital 4 oil industry 5 travel agents

3 03.06 **Listen and fill in the missing words.**

  a Was sind Sie von _____ ?
  b Ich _____ Finanzberater.
  c _____ arbeiten Sie?
  d Ich arbeite in _____ Bank in Frankfurt.
  e Sind _____ verheiratet? Ja.
  f _____ macht Ihre Frau?
  g _____ ist Krankenpflegerin.
  h Wo _____ sie?
  i Sie arbeitet in _____ Krankenhaus hier in Berlin.
  j Und Ihr Freund. Wo arbeitet _____ ?
  k Er _____ Student aber abends arbeitet er in _____ .

4 **Now prepare what you would say to answer the questions for yourself. Cover your answers and try to say them without looking.**

> Remember in German you do not use the article *a* when talking about your status or profession.

  a Was sind Sie von Beruf? Ich bin _____ .
  b Wo arbeiten Sie? Ich arbeite _____ .
  c Was macht Ihr Mann/Ihr Freund? Er ist _____ .
  d Wo arbeitet er? Er _____ .
  e Was macht Ihre Frau/Ihre Freundin. Sie ist _____ .
  f Wo arbeitet sie? Sie _____ .

Conversation

03.07 *Thorsten and Jane are still chatting in the hotel bar. Listen and follow the text. Then answer the question.*

1 What does Thorsten do? What does Jane do?

Thorsten	So was machst du hier in Berlin?
Jane	Ich gehe zu einem Musikkonzert.
Thorsten	Ja? Bist du Sängerin?
Jane	Nein! Ich bin Journalistin! Ich arbeite für eine Musikzeitschrift. Was machst du?
Thorsten	Ich arbeite als Webdesigner... in der Informationstechnologie.
Jane	Wie bitte?
Thorsten	Webdesigner... der Informationstechnologie. Computer ... Ich bin für die Messe hier.
Jane	Was ist das?
Thorsten	Eine Messe für die Informationstechnologieindustrie.
Jane	uhmmmm ... Möchtest du mit mir zum Konzert?
Thorsten	Wann?
Jane	Freitagabend.
Thorsten	Ich muss mal in meinen Kalender gucken ... Kalender ... Also, morgen ist... Donnerstag... Freitag... ja ... abends ist frei. Um wie viel Uhr?
Jane	ähm ... Um... 20 Uhr.
Thorsten	Dann haben wir Zeit zum Pizza essen. Isst du gern Pizza?
Jane	Ja, gerne... Gute Idee ...

 03.08 **Listen again and speak Jane's part.**

2 Review the expressions below from the conversation. Then match them to their English meaning.

a	Ich arbeite für eine Musikzeitschriften.	**i**	*When does the concert begin?*
b	Ich bin für die Messe hier.	**ii**	*Do you like pizza?*
c	Freitagabend.	**iii**	*I work for a music magazine.*
d	Wann beginnt das Konzert?	**iv**	*I am here for the trade fair.*
e	Isst du gern Pizza?	**v**	*Friday evening.*

Learn more

DER KALENDER *DAYS AND DATES*

 03.09 **Listen and repeat**

DIE TAGE DER WOCHE *THE DAYS OF THE WEEK*

Montag Dienstag Mittwoch Donnerstag Freitag Samstag Sonntag

There are actually two German words for *Saturday*. **Sonnabend** (literally '*sun eve*') is often used instead of **Samstag** in the north of Germany.

DIE MONATE *THE MONTHS*

Januar Februar März April Mai Juni Juli August September Oktober November Dezember

DIE ZAHLEN VON 20 BIS 100 *THE NUMBERS FROM 20 TO 100*

20 **zwanzig** *30* **dreißig** *40* **vierzig** *50* **fünfzig** *60* **sechzig** *70* **siebzig** *80* **achtzig** *90* **neunzig** *100* **hundert**

That was the easy bit! This is the harder bit:

21 **einundzwanzig** *22* **zweiundzwanzig** *23* **dreiundzwanzig**

In German, they say the units before the tens. Think of the nursery rhyme: four and twenty blackbirds baked in a pie.

Try saying these numbers:

25   36   42   53   61   74   88   99

PRACTICE

1 03.10 **When are they going to meet? Listen and link the day, date and month.**

Wir treffen uns... *We'll meet...*

Donnerstag	**31**	**Januar**
Montag	**24**	**März**
Freitag	**25**	**Mai**
Mittwoch	**15**	**Juli**
Sonntag	**22**	**August**
Dienstag	**18**	**September**
Samstag	**29**	**Oktober**

2 03.11 **Listen and write down the mobile numbers you hear.**

Wie ist Ihre Handynummer? *What's your mobile number?*

a _____

b _____

c _____

> Giving numbers people often say **zwo** instead of **zwei** as **zwei** can sound like **drei**.

3 **Give your phone number or mobile number:**
Meine Handynummer ist _____.

Reading and writing

1 **Read the texts and then answer the questions below. You don't need to understand every word to be able to answer them correctly.**

Mein Name ist Franz. Ich bin Geschäftsmann. Ich arbeite in einer Firma die Waschmachinen herstellt. Meine Frau Uta, ist im Moment arbeitslos, sie ist Optikerin, aber sie erwartet ein Baby.

Mein Freund Jörg ist Computerprogrammierer. Er arbeitet zu Hause. Seine Frau Elke arbeitet in einem Reisebüro.

Meine Freundin Hannelore ist Lehrerin. Ihr Mann Udo ist Geschäftsführer und arbeitet in einer großen Fabrik.

Who...

a works at home ?

b works in a washing machine factory?

c is a manager in a big factory ?

d works in a school ?

e works in a travel agency?

f is expecting a baby?

2 **Now write a text of your own using Franz's text as a pattern.**

 Test yourself

1 Fill in the missing words in the questions and answers.

    a Was sind Sie von _____?   Ich _____ Elektriker.

    b _____ arbeiten Sie?   In _____ Automobilfabrik.

    c Sind Sie _____?   Ja _____ Frau heißt Helga.

    d Was macht _____?   Sie _____ Sekretärin.

    e Wo _____ sie?   In _____ Büro.

2 Prepare answers to these questions for yourself and two friends.

    a Was sind Sie von Beruf?   Ich bin _____.

    b Wo arbeiten Sie?   In _____.

    c Was macht Ihr Freund?   Er ist _____.

    d Wo arbeitet er?   Er arbeitet _____.

    e Was macht Ihre Freundin?   Sie ist _____.

    f Wo arbeitet sie?   Sie arbeitet _____.

3 Say what time it is.

    a 8.15   **b** 9.20   **c** 10.30   **d** 12.45

    e 14.10   **f** 17.25   **g** 18.55   **h** 19.00

SELF CHECK	
I CAN. . .	
●	. . . say what I do and ask someone what they do
●	. . . say where I work and ask someone where they work
●	. . . say and recognize the days of the week
●	. . . say and recognize the months of the year
●	. . . say the numbers 20–100
●	. . . tell the time using the 24-hour clock

R1 *Review: Units 1–3*

1 **Imagine you are staying in a hotel in Germany and Herr Schuhmacher calls for you at 11 a.m. What would you say to him?**
   a Guten Morgen   b Guten Tag
   c Guten Abend   d Gute Nacht

2 **Match the German and the English.**
   a Ich heiße...   i *Well thanks, and you?*
   b Angenehm.   ii *Would you like a coffee?*
   c Wie geht's?   iii *I don't understand.*
   d Gut danke, und Ihnen?   iv *I'm called...*
   e Ich verstehe nicht.   v *Do you speak English?*
   f Sprechen Sie Englisch?   vi *Pleased to meet you.*
   g Trinken Sie einen Kaffee? vii *How are you?*

3 **There are two words for *you*: du and Sie. Which would you use?**
   a someone you don't know
   b if you are using first names
   c someone who is older than you
   d someone who is younger than you
   e someone to whom you want to show respect
   f a friend

4 **Write the grammar rule for the verb endings.**
   a after **du** the verb ends with
   b after **Sie** the verb ends with

5 **Imagine Herr Schuhmacher has come to see you. How would you ask him the following?**
   a *Would you like a coffee?*   i Ein Glas Wein?
   b *With milk and sugar?*   ii Trinken Sie einen Kaffee?
   c *A piece of cake?*   iii Mit Milch und Zucker?
   d *A glass of wine?*   iv Ein Stück Kuchen?

6 **Match the English to the German**

a *Yes, please.*
b *Pardon?*
c *I don't understand.*
d *No thanks.*
e *Is it OK?*
f *Don't mention it.*

i Nein danke.
ii Geht das?
iii Bitte, bitte.
iv Ja, gerne.
v Ich verstehe nicht.
vi Wie bitte?

7 **Write the grammar rule for *liking* and *preferring*.**
Fill in the missing words:
You use _____ to say you like something
and _____ to say you prefer it

a Ich esse _____ Käsekuchen – *I like cheesecake*
b Ich esse _____ Sahnetorte – *I prefer cream cake*
c Ich trinke _____ Rotwein – *I like red wine*
d Ich trinke _____ Weißwein – *I prefer white wine*

8 **Match the German to the English:**

a Sind Sie berufstätig?
b Ich bin persönlicher Assistant.
c Was macht Ihr Mann?
d Er ist Unternehmensberater.
e Was macht Ihre Frau?
f Sie ist Krankenpflegerin.
g Sie arbeitet in einem Krankenhaus.

i *She works in a hospital.*
ii *She's a nurse.*
iii *Do you work?*
iv *What does your husband do?*
v *He's a business consultant.*
vi *What does your wife do?*
vii *I'm a personal assistant.*

9 **Write the feminine form and the meaning of these job titles:**

Student _____   Krankenpfleger _____

Lehrer _____   Journalist _____

To make the feminine of most job titles you add _____

In German, when you say what someone else does you do not use '**a**' in front of the profession.

10 **Write the German for:**
a I am a manager. I work in a travel agents.
b He is a financial advisor. He works in a bank.
c She is a doctor. She works in a hospital.

Meine Familie und Freunde

My family and friends

In this unit, you will learn how to:
▶ *talk about yourself.*
▶ *say whether you are married or not.*
▶ *talk about your family and friends.*
▶ *describe yourself and other people.*
▶ *make simple comparisons.*

CEFR: (A1) *Can ask and answer questions about themselves and other people, where they live, people they know, things they have, etc.*

Familie und Verwandten *Family and relations*

For almost 90% of the population of Germany, **die Familie** is still considered the most important thing in their list of personal priorities. Most families now only have one or two **Kinder** *(children)* and about 65% of mothers are **berufstätig** *(in employment)*. When a German couple get **verlobt** *(engaged)* they usually exchange **Verlobungsringe** *(gold rings)* which they wear on the left hand. **Die Hochzeit** *(marriage)* is a civil ceremony but many couples also have a religious ceremony after the civil one. After the wedding the couples move their rings to the right hand to show they are now **verheiratet** *(married)*.

If the marriage fails, the couple might live **getrennt** *(separated)* or they might get **geschieden** *(divorced)*. Many couples nowadays just live together in a **Lebensgemeinschaft** *(partnership)* and call each other **Lebenspartner/partnerin** or **Lebensabschnittpartner/partnerin** instead of **Mann** *(husband)* **und Frau** *(wife)*.

Find the words in the text that mean:

wedding _____   *separated* _____
married _____   *divorced* _____
engaged _____

Vocabulary builder

04.01 Look at the words and phrases and complete the missing English expressions. Then listen to these words and see if any sound like English words you know. Cover up the English and see if you can remember what they mean.

meine Familie	*my family*
mein Vater	*my father*
meine Mutter	_____
meine Eltern	*my parents*
mein Bruder	_____
meine Schwester	*my sister*
mein Sohn	_____
meine Tochter	_____
meine Kinder	*my children*
mein Großvater (Opa)	*my grandfather*
meine Großmutter (Oma)	_____
meine Großeltern	_____
mein Mann	*my husband*
meine Frau	*my wife*

Vocabulary to describe what someone is like. *He/she is:* **Er/sie ist:**

groß *big/tall*	**klein** *small*
schön *nice/beautiful*	**hübsch** *pretty*
faul *lazy*	**fleißig** *hard-working*
laut *noisy/sporty*	**ruhig** *calm/quiet*
jung *young*	**alt** *old*
schlank *thin*	**dick** *fat*

Because most people are not wholly one thing or another it might be useful to learn these modifiers:

ganz *quite*   **sehr** *very*   **zu** *too*

Conversation

 04.02 *John and Herr Schuhmacher are sitting in the bar and talking. Listen and follow the text. Then choose the correct answer.*

1 What are they discussing?

a jobs   b wives   c children

Herr Schuhmacher	Haben Sie Kinder?
John	Noch nicht. Und Sie?
Herr Schuhmacher	Ja... ich habe einen Sohn, Stefan, und eine Tochter, Silke.
John	Und was macht ihr Sohn?
Herr Schuhmache	ähm ... er geht noch in die Schule.
John	Wie ist er sonst?
Herr Schuhmacher	Er ist ein normaler Siebzehnjähriger, zu laut, spielt mit dem Computer, schickt immer SMS und flirtet mit Mädchen.
John	Also ganz normal! Und was macht Ihre Tochter?
Herr Schuhmacher	Silke? Sie ist Studentin und geht auf die Uni, hier in Berlin.
John	Und wie ist sie?
Herr Schuhmacher	Sie ist... fleissig ... ja, und hübsch.
John	Ja? ... und was studiert sie?
Herr Schuhmacher	Zahn Medizin. Sie will Zahnärztin werden.
John	Das wäre nichts für mich!
Herr Schuhmacher	Für mich auch nicht!

04.03 **Listen again and speak John's part.**

2 Find the expressions in the conversation.

   a Have you got children? _____.
   b Not yet. _____.
   c What's he like? _____.
   d Too loud. _____.
   e That's not for me. _____.
   f Not for me either. _____.

3 Match the questions and answers.

   a Und was macht Ihr Sohn?   **i**   Sie geht auf die Uni.
   b Wie ist er sonst?   **ii**   Sie ist fleissig.
   c Und was macht Ihre Tochter?   **iii** Er geht noch in die Schule.
   d Und wie ist sie?   **iv**   Er ist normaler Siebzehnjähriger.

ⓘ Language discovery

TALKING ABOUT SOMEONE ELSE: *HE* AND *SHE*

1. **Look at the conversation. How do you say the following?**

   a He is _____
   d She is _____

   b He plays _____
   e She goes _____

   c He flirts _____
   f She studies _____

2 **Mein or meine? Fill in the blanks with mein or meine. Not sure? Look at the text and Vocabulary builder.**

   a _____ Sohn
   e _____ Frau
   i _____ Großeltern

   b _____ Tochter
   f _____ Freund
   j _____ Oma

   c _____ Bruder
   g _____ Schwester
   k _____ Mann

   d _____ Eltern
   h _____ Kinder
   l _____ Freundin

3 **Choose the right word.**

   a You use **mein** in front of masc/fem/plural nouns.
   b You use **meine** in front of masc/fem/plural nouns.

> The word for *he* is **er** and the word for *she* is **sie**. After *he* and *she* the verb ends in **-t**.

Learn more

In German, we use these subject pronouns:

er *he*   **sie** *she*   **sie** *they*

In German, **sie** can mean *she* or *they*. Confusing? Check the verb – if the verb ends in **-t**, it means *she*.

To describe someone, you say:

er ist *he is*   **sie ist** *she is*   **sie sind** *they are*

Er ist ganz groß. *He is quite big.*

Sie ist sehr hübsch. *She is very pretty.*

Sie sind sehr alt. *They are very old.*

 PRACTICE

1 **Choose the right word.**

   a Er geht in die Schule. *(he/she/they)*

   b Sie gehen in die Schule. *(he/she/they)*

   c Sie geht auf die Uni. *(he/she/they)*

   d Sie spielen Tennis. *(he/she/they)*

   e Er spielt Rugby. *(he/she/they)*

   f Sie spielt Golf. *(he/she/they)*

Listen and learn

 1 04.04 **Listen to Frau Schuhmacher talk about her relations. What are the correct roman numerals for the words? (Don't worry if you don't understand every word!)**

| i husband | ii mother | iii father | iv parents |
| v daughter | vi son | vii grandmother |

a _____ b _____ c _____ d _____
e _____ f _____ g _____

2 04.05 **Who is Herr Schuhmacher talking about? Listen and fill in the missing words from the box.**

| Vater | Frau | Tochter | Sohn | Oma |

a Mein _____ ist ganz groß.
b Meine _____ ist sehr hübsch.
c Meine _____ ist ganz schlank.
d Mein _____ ist sehr alt.
e Meine _____ ist klein und ruhig.

3 04.06 **Match the people and their descriptions.**

a Jens   i quite fat and calm
b Heike   ii pretty but lazy
c Silke   iii quite small and pretty
d Jörg   iv tall and thin
e Uta   v big and nice
f Hannelore   vi very big and too loud

4 Prepare two things to say about:
a yourself. **Ich bin** _____
b a masculine friend or relation. **Er ist** _____
c a feminine friend or relation. **Sie ist** _____

Conversation

04.07 *Jane and Thorsten are in the pizzeria. Listen and follow the text. Then choose the correct answer.*

1 What are they talking about?
  a what they like to eat
  b their jobs
  c other people

Thorsten	Schmeckt's?
Jane	Ja, schmeckt gut und wie ist es mit der Pasta?
Thorsten	Ja, schmeckt. Entschuldigung... eine SMS von meinem Bruder. Er kommt morgen Vormitttag in Berlin an.
Jane	Dein Bruder? Woher kommt er?
Thorsten	Aus Amerika.
Jane	Mmmmmm! Wie ist er?
Thorsten	Er ist größer als ich, und dicker.
Jane	Ist er älter oder jünger?
Thorsten	Älter... Er ist 28 Jahre alt.
Jane	Ahm ... Und hast du noch andere Geschwister?
Thorsten	Ja, eine jüngere Schwester. Sie ist 20 Jahre alt und studiert in Hamburg.
Jane	Wie ist sie sonst?
Thorsten	ähm ... Also ... sie ist kleiner als ich, schlank und hübsch. Sie hat blonde Haare und blaue Augen. Sieh mal. Ich habe ein Foto auf meinem Handy.
Jane	Wer ist der andere Mann?
Thorsten	Das ist ihr Freund.
Jane	Hmm. Er ist sehr groß.
Thorsten	Hast du Geschwister?
Jane	Ja, eine Schwester. Sie ist verheiratet, hat zwei Kinder und wohnt auch in Amerika, in Miami.
Thorsten	Mein Bruder wohnt auch in Miami.
Jane	Welch ein Zufall!

04.08 **Listen and speak Jane's part.**

2 **Read the conversation again and choose the correct meanings.**

   a Woher kommt er?
   - **i** *What colour hair has he got?*
   - **ii** *Where is he coming from?*
   - **iii** *Where is he going to?*

   b ein Foto auf meinen Handy
   - **i** *a picture on my mobile*
   - **ii** *a picture on my laptop*
   - **iii** *a picture on my handycam*

   c Wer ist der andere Mann?
   - **i** *Where is the other man?*
   - **ii** *Who is the other man?*
   - **iii** *How is the other man?*

   d Welch ein Zufall!
   - **i** *What an accident!*
   - **ii** *What a bad fall!*
   - **iii** *What a coincidence!*

Language discovery

1 **In German, there is one word for brothers and sisters. Find the phrase in the text which means:**

   Do you have (more) brothers and sisters?

2 **Find the phrases in the text that mean:**
   a He is taller than me and fatter.
   b Is he older or younger than you?
   c She is smaller than I (am).

Learn more

MAKING COMPARISONS

It is easy to make comparisons in German as it is done in the same way as in English. Add **-er** to the end of the adjective: **klein – kleiner** *(small/smaller)*

If the preceding vowel is an **a, o**, or **u** it will take an **Umlaut**;

lang – länger *(long/longer)*; **alt – älter** *(old/older)*; **jung – jünger** *(young/younger)*.

Er ist größer als ich. *He is bigger/taller than me.*

Sie ist kleiner als ich. *She is smaller than me.*

DESCRIBING PEOPLE

Ich bin Er ist Sie ist	**ganz** *quite* **ziemlich** *rather* **sehr** *very* **zu** *too*		**groß** *big/tall* **mittelgroß** *average size* **klein** *small* **fleißig** *hard-working*
Ich habe Er hat Sie hat	**lange** *long* **kurze** *short* **blonde** *blond* **braune** *brown*		**Haare** *hair*
	blaue *blue* **dunkle** *dark*		**Augen** *eyes*
Ich bin	**größer/ kleiner jünger/älter**	**als**	**mein Freund meine Freundin**

 PRACTICE

1 **Use the information in the chart and prepare what you would say to describe yourself to someone over the phone. Compare yourself to someone in your family or a friend.**

 2 **Imagine you have a black and white photo of your wife/husband/ friend which you are showing to Thorsten. Tell him about the person in the photo. Include the following information:**

   a Say who it is. Das ist mein/meine _____.

   b Say what sort of person he/she is. Er/sie ist _____.

   c Say what colour hair and eyes he/she has. Er/sie hat _____.

   d Make a comparison with yourself. Er/sie ist _____ als ich.

Reading and writing

 1 **Read the letter below. Can you figure out the meaning of the following words?**

   a Musiker
   b verlobt
   c Hochzeit

Liebe Nathalie

Du fragst mich nach meiner Familie. Also… mein Vater ist größer als ich und meine Mutter ist kleiner. Sie hat blonde Haare und blaue Augen. Mein Bruder ist siebzehn Jahre alt und faul. Er ist groß und dick und sitzt den ganzen Tag vor dem Computer und spielt Computerspiele. Meine Schwester ist mittelgroß und hat lange dunkle Haare. Sie ist ganz hübsch und fleißig. Sie studiert Biologie in Berlin und ihr Freund ist Musiker und spielt Gitarre und singt. Sie sind verlobt. Ihre Hochzeit ist im Juni.   Wie ist deine Familie?

Tschüs, Jörg

2 **Answer the questions.**
   a Who has blond hair?
   b Who has dark hair?
   c Who is lazy?
   d Who is hard-working?
   e Who plays the guitar?
   f When is the wedding?

 3 **Now write a similar text about your family or friends using Jörg's text as a model.**

 Test yourself

 1 04.09 **Listen and choose the correct word.**

    a Lars is big/small/average.

    b He has blonde/brown/dark hair and blue/brown eyes.

    c He is sporty/lazy/hard-working.

    d He likes playing tennis/football.

    e He is married/unmarried.

    f He has a son/daughter.

2 **Write a paragraph about yourself.**

3 **Now write something about two other people. Use the listening material as a model.**

Er/Sie heißt _____

Er/Sie ist _____

Er/Sie hat _____

SELF CHECK

	I CAN...
○	... talk about myself
○	... say whether I am married or not
○	... talk about other people: family and friends
○	... describe myself and other people
○	... make simple comparisons

5 *Eine Stadtrundfahrt*
A tour of the town

In this unit, you will learn how to:
▶ *say the names of places in a town.*
▶ *ask for directions.*
▶ *understand directions.*
▶ *give simple directions.*
▶ *recognize whether a noun is masculine, feminine or neuter.*
▶ *build new German words.*

CEFR: (A1) *Can understand questions and instructions addressed carefully and slowly to him/ her and follow short, simple directions. Can ask for and give directions referring to a map or plan.*

Die Stadt *The town*

Before unification in 1871, Germany was made up of over 300 principalities, each with its own **Hauptstadt** *(main town)* and **Schloß** or **Burg** *(fortified castle)*. These were often situated on a **Berg** *(hill/ mountain)* overlooking a **Fluß** *(river)* at a suitable crossing place and a **Brücke** *(bridge)* which could also be guarded. Because the rulers often quarrelled, people preferred to live in the relative safety of the towns, which is why there are so many towns in Germany. Each town had a **Rathaus** *(town hall)*, a **Marktplatz** *(a market place)* and a **Kirche** *(church)* or **Dom** *(a cathedral)*. A lot of Germany's new towns are based around the core of the old town. You will often find a **Schloß oder Burg, Fluß** and **Brücke** at the heart of a town but now you will also usually find a **Museum** *(museum)*, a **Bibliothek** *(a library)* a **Universität** *(university)* and a **Kunstgallerie** or **Pinakothek** *(two words for art gallery)*, and, of course, the modern **Einkaufszentrum** *(shopping centre)*.

What feature are these towns named after?
Hamburg   Osnabrück   Neunkirchen   Heidelberg

Vocabulary builder

05.01 **In German, many of the names for places in a town look or sound like their English equivalent. Look at these and try to figure out what they mean. Write the missing expressions. Then listen and see if any sound like English words you know. Cover up the English and see if you can remember what they mean.**

> In German, all nouns are masculine, feminine or neuter.
>
> masculine **der Bahnhof** *(station)*
> feminine **die Bank** *(bank)*
> neuter **das Rathaus** *(town hall)*

PLACES IN A TOWN

in der Stadt	*in the town*
der Bahnhof	*station*
der Hauptbahnhof	*the main station*
die Bank	_____
der Flughafen	_____
das Hotel	_____
das Informationsbüro	_____
das Kino	_____
das Krankenhaus	*the hospital*
die Messe	*the trade fair*
das Restaurant	_____
die Straße	*the street*
die Hauptstraße	_____
das Theater	_____

NEW EXPRESSIONS

Wie komme ich zum Hotel ?	*How do I get to the _____?*
Wo ist die Bushaltestelle?	*Where is the _____?*
Wie oft fährt der Bus?	*How often does the _____ go?*
Ist es weit?	*Is it far?*

RICHTUNGEN – *DIRECTIONS*

Sie gehen hier links/rechts/geradeaus	*You go left/right/straight*
die erste Straße links	*left at the first street*
und die nächste Straße rechts	*and right at the next*
und (das Hotel) ist auf der rechten/ linken Seite.	*the (hotel) is on the right/ left (side).*

Conversation

 05.02 *John is talking to Frau Braun. Listen and follow the text. Then choose the correct answer.*

1 Where do you think they are?

    a in the information office   **b** at the airport   **c** in the street

Frau Braun	Guten Tag.
John	Guten Tag.
Frau Braun	Wie kann ich Ihnen helfen?
John	Bitte, wo ist das Hotel Europa?
Frau Braun	Hotel Europa? ... Ja... es ist in der Hauptstraße.
John	Ist es weit von hier?
Frau Braun	Nein, nicht weit... etwa fünf Minuten.
John	Wie komme ich zum Hotel?
Frau Braun	Hier, sehen Sie auf dem Plan... Sie gehen hier links und dann... Sie sind in der Hauptstraße... und das Hotel ist 100m auf der rechten Seite.
John	Und wie komme ich zum Flughafen?
Frau Braun	Der Flughafen? Also... am besten fahren Sie mit dem Bus, dem Pendelbus.
John	Wie oft fährt der Bus ?
Frau Braun	Er fährt alle zwanzig Minuten.
John	Wo ist die Haltestelle?
Frau Braun	Die Haltestelle ist vor dem Hauptbahnhof.
John	Vielen Dank.
Frau Braun	Nichts zu danken. Gern geschehen.

05.03 Listen and speak John's part.

2 Match the questions and answers.

    a Wo ist das Hotel Europa?   **i**   Nein, nicht weit.

    b Ist es weit von hier?   **ii** Alle zwanzig Minuten.

    c Wie komme ich   **iii** Vor dem Hauptbahnhof.

       zum Flughafen?   **iv** Mit dem Bus.

    d Wo ist die Haltestelle?   **v**   In der Hauptstraße.

    e Wie oft fährt der Bus?

3 **What do you think? Read the conversation and answer the questions below.**

   a Where does John want to go to first?

   b Where does Frau Braun say it is?

   c Is it far?

   d On what side is it?

   e Where does John ask the way to next?

   f How should he get there?

 # Language discovery

1 **Find the expressions in the conversation.**

   a How can I help you?

   b in the main street

   c Is it far?

   d It's best to go by bus.

   e You go left here.

   f It goes every 20 minutes.

   g in front of the main station

   h Don't mention it.

Now cover up your answers and see if you can say them without looking at the conversation

2 **Which words from the conversation mean the same as the expressions below?**

   a You go left here.

   b You go by bus.

Learn more

GENDER OF NOUNS

In German, all nouns are masculine, feminine or neuter.

When you look a noun up it will usually have (*m*), (*f*) or (*n*) after it to tell you which gender it is.

The word for *the* changes according to the gender of the noun.

(m) words are masculine, or **der** words   **der Bahnhof** – *the station*

(f) words are feminine, or **die** words   **die Kirche** – *the church*

(n) words are neuter, or **das** words   **das Rathaus** – *the town hall*

Nouns which are made up of two words always take the gender of the *latter* part of the word:

die Information + das Büro = das Informationsbüro

ZUM AND ZUR

When asking for directions, you use **zum** with masculine and neuter nouns and **zur** with feminine nouns.

Wie komme ich zum Hotel?   *How do I get to the hotel?*

Wie komme ich zur Brücke?   *How do I get to the bridge?*

GEHEN AND FAHREN

Gehen and **fahren** both mean *to go*. You use **gehen** if you are going on foot but you use **fahren** if you are going by transport, even on rollerskates, a bicycle or even on skis.

Ich gehe zu Fuß.   *I am walking/going on foot.*

Ich fahre mit dem Bus/Zug/Auto. *I am going by bus/train/car.*

▶ You may have noticed that in the dialogue **die Straße** becomes **in der Straße**.

Don't worry about it yet. Just try to memorize the phrases: **mit dem Bus, in der Straße, zum Bahnhof** and **zur Brücke** and use them as patterns.

1 Look at these new words from the introductory reading in this unit. Put **der**, **die** or **das** in front of each word. Then write the meaning after it. The (*m*), (*f*) or (*n*) tells you whether the noun is a masculine, feminine or neuter word.

a _____ Berg (m) _____   **b** _____ Bibliothek (f) _____

c _____ Brücke (f) _____   **d** _____ Burg (f) _____

e _____ Dom (m) _____   **f** _____ Einkaufszentrum (n) _____

g _____ Fluß (m) _____   **h** _____ Hauptstadt (f) _____

i _____ Kirche (f) _____   **j** _____ Kunstgallerie (f) _____

k _____ Marktplatz (m) _____   **l** _____ Museum (n) _____

m _____ Rathaus (n) _____   **n** _____ Schloß (n) _____

2 Word building. Use what you already know and the words in the box to help you make new words.

a the capital or main town

b the main station

c the main street

d the town plan

e the town centre

3 What do you think these words mean?

a die Straßenbahn

b die U-Bahn (Untergrundbahn)

c die Autobahn

Nouns which are made up of two words always take the gender of the *latter* part of the word.

haupt – *main*

die Bahn – *way (as in railway)*

die Stadt – *town*

die Straße – *street*

---

4 Fill in the blanks with **zum/zur**.
Wie komme ich _____?

a _____ Bahnhof?

b _____ Schloß?

c _____ Museum?

d _____ Stadtzentrum?

e _____ Autobahn?

f _____ Flughafen?

> Did you notice? They were mostly ——, so when in doubt, use it!

Listen and learn

1 05.04 **Listen and write the number of the correct picture. Where do they want to go? You do not need to understand every word to do the exercise.**

a ☐   b ☐   c ☐   d ☐   e ☐
i   ii   iii   iv   v

2 05.04 **Listen again and write the letter of the correct speech bubble. What are they told?**

a ☐   b ☐   c ☐   d ☐   e ☐
i   ii   iii   iv   v

I don't know   Take the bus   On the right   At the station   In the main street

Conversation

05.05 *Jane and Thorsten are chatting in the bar. Thorsten asks Jane about her plans. Listen and follow the text.*

1 What is Jane planning to do on Saturday?

a go to a concert	b visit the sights	c she doesn't know

Thorsten	So was machst du am Samstag?
Jane	Ich weiß noch nicht. Was machst du?
Thorsten	Ich gehe zum Fernsehturm. Kommst du mit?
Jane	Gerne. Wo treffen wir uns?
Thorsten	Vor dem Eingang.
Jane	Wie komme ich zum Turm?
Thorsten	Am besten mit dem Bus.
Jane	Wo ist die Haltestelle?
Thorsten	Vor dem Hotel Stein. Du gehst links und die Haltestelle ist auf der rechten Seite.
Jane	Um wie viel Uhr?
Thorsten	So, um halb zwölf. Dann können wir im Restaurant essen.
Jane	Ja schön... Und dein Bruder?
Thorsten	... morgen leidet er sicher an Jetlag ...
Jane	Schade!

05.06 **Listen again and speak Jane's part.**

2 Review the expressions below from the conversation. Then match them to the English meaning.

a Kommst du mit?   i *About half past eleven.*
b Wo treffen wir uns?   ii *What a pity!*
c So, um halb zwölf.   iii *He's sure to have jetlag.*
d Leidet er sicher an Jetlag. iv *Where (shall) we meet?*
e Schade!   v *Would you like to come with me?*

3 Match the questions and answers.

a Was machst du?   i Vor dem Eingang.
b Kommst du mit?   ii Am besten mit dem Bus.
c Um wie viel Uhr?   iii Gerne.
d Wie komme ich zum Turm?   iv So um halb zwölf.
e Wo treffen wir uns?   v Ich gehe zum Fernsehturm.

 Language discovery

German is a very logical language. **Eingang** is *entrance* if you are going in on foot. **Einfahrt** is *entrance* if you are driving in.

Ausgang is *exit on foot*, so can you figure out the word for *exit* on a motorway?

> **Gang** is from the verb **gehen** *(to go)* and we use it in the expression **gangplank** for going onto a boat.

 PRACTICE

1   **Look at the map, read the advice and figure out where these people want to go.**

   a   Sie gehen hier geradeaus, über die Brücke und es ist auf dem Berg. Sie können es nicht verfehlen!

   b   Sie fahren hier geradeaus, an der Ampel rechts und dann immer geradeaus.

   c   Sie fahren immer geradeaus, über die Brücke und dann die erste Straße links. Er ist auf der rechten Seite.

2   **Find the phrases in the text which mean:**

   a   right at the lights

   b   over the bridge

   c   you go (always) straight

   d   You can't miss it!

   e   the first street on the left

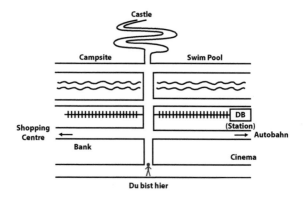

Reading and writing

 Read the information and write down the letter from the map.

i Das Informationsbüro ist nur zwei Minuten von hier, auf der rechten Seite.

ii Die U-Bahnstation ist am Marktplatz. Sie nehmen die zweite Straße links und dann gehen Sie immer geradeaus.

iii Sie nehmen die zweite Strasse rechts, über die Brücke und dann rechts. Der Parkplatz ist auf der linken Seite.

iv Gehen Sie hier geradeaus bis zur Ampel und dann links und das Einkaufszentrum ist auf der rechten Seite

v Das Hotel ist in der Hauptstraße, neben der U-Bahnstation.

 Now write notes explaining to someone how to get to:

1 the station
2 the airport
3 the hospital

Giving advice		
	Sie	**du**
you go	Sie gehen	du gehst
you drive	Sie fahren	du fährst

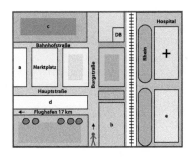

? Test yourself

1 **Ask where these places are. Wo ist...?**

a _____

b  _____

c  _____

d  _____

2 **Ask how to get to the places in Exercise 1.**

Wie komme ich zum/zur...

a Wie komme ich _____ _____?

b Wie komme ich _____ _____?

c Wie komme ich _____ _____?

d Wie komme ich _____ _____?

3 **Match the phrases with the English meaning.**

a Sie gehen hier rechts.
b Die erste Straße links.
c Auf der rechten Seite.
d Sie gehen geradeaus.
e Es ist nicht weit.
f Gehen Sie mit dem Bus.

i *You go straight.*
ii *It's not far.*
iii *Go by bus.*
iv *Go right.*
v *It's on the right.*
vi *The first on the left.*

4 **How would you ask where these places are?**

Wo ist... ?

a the bank
b the bridge
c the town hall
d the station
e the castle

5 How would you ask the way to these well-known Berlin landmarks? **Wie komme ich zum/zur...?**

   a der Fernsehturm *(television tower)*
   b die Berliner Mauer *(the Berlin Wall)*
   c der Reichstag *(the parliament)*
   d das Brandenburger Tor *(Brandenburg Gate)*
   e die Gedächtniskirche *(the memorial church)*

SELF CHECK

	I CAN. . .
●	. . . say the names of places in a town
●	. . . ask for directions
●	. . . understand directions
●	. . . give simple directions
●	. . . recognize whether a noun is masculine, feminine or neuter
●	. . . build new German words

6 Das Hotel
The hotel

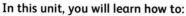

In this unit, you will learn how to:
▶ *book a room in a hotel.*
▶ *give personal details.*
▶ *spell your name.*
▶ *ask about facilities.*
▶ *say 'not a'.*

CEFR: (A1) *Can interact with reasonable ease in structured sentences, using numbers and dates, names, nationality, address, age, date of birth or arrival in the country, and deal with events such as booking into a hotel.*

Unterkünfte in Deutschland
Accommodation in Germany

There is a broad range of accommodation available in Germany from the relatively cheap **Pension** *(guest house)* to the **Luxus-Hotel** *(luxury hotel)*. At the top end is the **5-Sterne-Hotel** *(five star hotel)* where you can expect **Mini-bar, Klimaanlage** *(air conditioning)*, **Internetanschluss oder WIFI im Zimmer** *(internet connection or wifi in the room)*, and **Wellness oder Spa, Schwimmbad** *(pool)* and **Fitnessraum** *(fitness suite)*.

A **Gasthaus** *(inn)* is usually family owned. You can expect it to have its own restaurant which is open to non-residents. A **Hotel Garni** only provides **Übernachtung mit Frühstück** *(overnight with breakfast)*.

A **Pension** is a more modest accommodation which offers **Bett und Frühstück** *(bed and breakfast)* and sometimes **Abendessen** *(dinner)*, but not usually to non-residents.

 Abendessen is an evening meal. What do you think the word *for lunch (at midday)* is? _____

Vocabulary builder

06.01 Look at the words and phrases and complete the missing English expressions. Then listen to these words and see if any sound like English words you know. Cover up the English and see if you can remember what they mean.

UNTERKÜNFTE *ACCOMMODATION*

das Zimmer	*the room*
ein Einzelzimmer	*a single room*
ein Doppelzimmer	_____
ein Zimmer mit Bad	_____
ein Zimmer mit Dusche	_____
der Eingang	*the entrance*
der Ausgang	_____
der Notausgang	*emergency exit*
die Toilette	_____
der Empfang	*reception*
der Empfangstisch	*reception desk*
die Empfangsdame	_____
der Empfangsherr	_____
der Fahrstuhl/der Lift	*the lift*
die Treppe	*the stairs*
der Stock	*floor/storey*
der Schlüssel	*the key*

NEW EXPRESSIONS

Fill in the missing words.

Haben Sie ein Zimmer frei?	*Have you (got) a room?*
Wie viele Personen?	*How many _____?*
Wie viele Nächte?	*How many _____?*
Wie lange bleiben Sie?	*How _____ are you staying?*
Wir haben keinen Fitnessraum.	*We haven't got a _____ room.*
Gibt es Internetanschluss?	*Is there _____ connection?*
Es gibt keine Funkverbindung.	*There is no reception.*

Conversation

 06.02 *John is booking into a hotel for the weekend. Listen and follow the text. Then answer the question.*

1 How long is John staying?

Empfangsdame	Guten Abend.
John	Guten Abend.
Empfangsdame	Haben Sie eine Reservierung?
John	Nein. Haben Sie noch ein Zimmer frei?
Empfangsdame	Einzelzimmer oder Doppelzimmer?
John	Einzelzimmer.
Empfangsdame	Ja, wie lange bleiben Sie?
John	Zwei Nächte.
Empfangsdame	Mit Bad oder mit Dusche?
John	Mit Bad. Wie viel kostet es?
Empfangsdame	48 Euros.
John	Und was kostet ein Zimmer mit Dusche?
Empfangsdame	45 Euros.
John	Mit Frühstück?
Empfangsdame	Ja, inklusive ein Frühstück.
John	Ich nehme das Zimmer mit Dusche. Gibt es einen Fitnessraum?
Empfangsdame	Leider nicht. Wir haben keinen Fitnessraum.
John	Wo kann ich hier parken?
Empfangsdame	Hinter dem Hotel. Hier ist der Schlüssel, Zimmer 307 im dritten Stock.
John	Gibt es einen Fahrstuhl?
Empfangsdame	Ja, dort drüben. Würden Sie sich bitte eintragen?

06.03 **Now listen again and say John's part.**

2 Match the questions and answers.

a Wie lange bleiben Sie?   i   Hinter dem Hotel.
b Mit Bad oder mit Dusche?   ii Zwei Nächte.
c Wie viel kostet es?   iii Ja, dort drüben.
d Wo kann ich hier parken?   iv 48 Euros.
e Gibt es einen Fitnessraum? v   Mit Bad.
f Gibt es einen Fahrstuhl?   vi Wir haben keinen Fitnessraum.

3 **What do you think? Read the conversation and answer the questions below.**

    a Has John booked a room?

    b What sort of room does he want ?

    c How is he travelling?

    d What floor is his room on?

    e What does she ask him to do?

 Language discovery

1 **Match the expressions to the meanings.**

a Wie lange bleiben Sie?	**i**	*Have you got a room free?*
b Inklusive Frühstück.	**ii**	*How much does it cost?*
c Wo kann ich hier parken?	**iii**	*How long are you staying?*
d Wie viel kostet es?	**iv**	*Including breakfast.*
e Im dritten Stock.	**v**	*Where can I park?*
f Haben Sie ein Zimmer frei?	**vi**	*Behind the hotel.*
g Hinter dem Hotel.	**vii**	*Over there.*
h Dort drüben.	**viii**	*On the third floor.*

Now cover up your answers and see if you can say them without looking at the conversation.

2 **Which words from the conversation mean the same as the expressions below?**

    a How much?

    b How long?

Learn more

There are two ways of asking questions. You can ask a question starting with a verb (*Have you...? Are/Is...?*) or with a question word (*What? Why? How?*).

QUESTIONS STARTING WITH A VERB

Haben Sie....? *Have you (got)....?*

Haben Sie Funkverbindung? *Have you got a mobile connection?*

Gibt es.... ? *Are/Is there...?* (**Gibt** comes from the verb **geben** – *to give*.)

Gibt es Internetanschluss? *Is there an internet connection?*

QUESTIONS STARTING WITH A QUESTION WORD

Wie lange? *How long?*

Wie viele Nächte? *How many nights?*

Wie viel kostet es? *How much does it cost?*

KEIN

Kein is a special word for *not a.*

It follows the same pattern as **ein** *(a)* and **mein** *(my).*

	masculine	feminine	neuter	plural
a	ein	ein	ein	
my	mein	meine	mein	meine
not a	kein	keine	kein	keine

Keine Zeit! *No time!*

Kein Geld! *No money!*

Kein Glück! *No luck!*

Wir haben keinen Fitnessraum. *We haven't got a gym room.*

Es gibt keine Funkverbindung. *There is no signal.*

Es gibt keinen Internetanschluss. *There's no internet connection.*

After **haben** and **es gibt**, the masculine form adds **-n**.

Gibt es einen Fitnessraum? Nein, es gibt keinen Fitnessraum.

Haben Sie einen Bruder? Nein, ich habe keinen Bruder.

 PRACTICE

1 Give the German for the following.
   a Have you got an internet connection?
   b Is there a lift?
   c How many people?
   d How long are you staying?
   e Have you got a fitness room?
   f Is there mobile reception?

2 How would you say:
   a I haven't got a sister.
   b He hasn't got a car.
   c She hasn't got a brother.
   d He has no money.
   e I have no mobile connection.

Listen and Learn

It is a good idea to learn the names of the letters in German and how to spell many of the words you may need. This will be useful in situations such as booking a car by phone where you will have to give your name and address. The alphabet is quite easy as it is very similar to the English alphabet. Just concentrate on the letters that are different.

3 06.04 **Das Alphabet** *The alphabet*

a – ah   b – bay   c – tsay   d – day   e – ay   f – eff   g – gay

h – hah   i – ee   j – yot   k – kah   l – ell   m – emm   n – enn

o – oh   p – pay   q – koo   r – air   s – es   t – tay   u – ooh

v – fow   w – vay   x – icks   y – ipsilon   z – tset

ä – eh   äu – oy   ö – er   ü – euh   ß – ess

nn = doppel n

ß = s tset or scharfes s

These letters are not what you would expect so pay special attention to them:

a – ah   e – ay   i – ee   v – fow   w – vay

> An easy way to remember v and w is to learn the abbreviation for Volkswagen cars: **VW** is **fow-vay** in German!

- ▶ **Practise saying the alphabet (after the recording if possible) and check your pronunciation.**
- ▶ **Write down the sound of the letters you need to spell your own name and learn them off by heart.**
- ▶ **Wie schreibt man das?** How do you spell it? (*lit. how does one write it?*)

3 06.05 **What are their names?**

a _____

b _____

c _____

d _____

e _____

4 06.06 **Where do they live?**

a _____

b _____

c _____

d _____

e _____

5 06.07 **Listen and fill in the answer grid.**

	Type of room	Length of stay
a		
b		
c		
d		
e		

6 06.08 **Read the conversation. Write what you are going to say and then say it out loud. Then listen to the recording and say your part in the pauses.**

Guten Abend.

Say good evening.

Wie kann ich Ihnen helfen?

Ask if they have a room.

Einzelzimmer oder Doppelzimmer?

You choose.

Wie lange bleiben Sie?

Say how long you want to stay.

Mit Bad oder mit Dusche?

You choose.

Ja, wir haben ein Zimmer.

Ask how much it costs.

48 Euro.

Ask if that is with breakfast.

Ja, Frühstück ist inbegriffen.

Ask where you can park the car.

Es gibt ein Parkhaus gegenüber dem Hotel.

Say you're sorry, you don't understand.

She indicates the multi-storey car park across the road and gives you a token for it.

Say thank you.

Nichts zu danken.

Conversation

 06.09 *Jane is booking into a hotel at the airport. Listen and follow the text. Then answer the questions.*

1 What is her room number? What floor is her room on?

Jane	Ich habe ein Zimmer reserviert.
Empfangsdame	Wie ist Ihr Name?
Jane	Smith.
Empfangsdame	Und Ihr Vorname?
Jane	Jane.
Empfangsdame	Wie schreibt man das?
Jane	J A N E.
Empfangsdame	Wie ist Ihre Adresse?
Jane	42 High Street,...
Empfangsdame	Wie ist die Postleitzahl?
Jane	NW3 7EV.
Empfangsdame	Geburtsort?
Jane	London, England.
Empfangsdame	Haben Sie eine Handynummer?
Jane	0 7 2 3 4 2 2 6 4 7 5
Empfangsdame	Und die Vorwahl?
Jane	0044.
Empfangsdame	Ich muß Ihre Kreditkarte durchziehen.
Jane	Bitte schön.
Empfangsdame	Also... Zimmer Nummer 407 im vierten Stock.
Jane	Gibt es einen Fahrstuhl?
Empfangsdame	Dort drüben. Hier ist der Schlüssel.
Jane	Danke.
Empfangsdame	Bitte, bitte.

2 How does the receptionist ask the following?
   a What is your family name?
   b What is your first name?
   c How you spell it?
   d What is your address?
   e What is your postal code?
   f Have you got a mobile number?

# Language discovery

1 **Which phrases from the conversation mean the same as these expressions?**
   a place of birth
   b I've got to swipe your credit card.

Learn more

Im welchen Stock? *On what floor?*

When you say what floor or storey a room is on, you use ordinal numbers (first, second, third etc.).

Ordinal numbers are easy in German because you just add -te to the number. The only exceptions are *1st* and *3rd*.

1st	**erste**
2nd	**zweite**
3rd	**dritte**
4th	**vierte**
5th	**fünfte**
on the ground floor	**im Erdgeshoß**

Practice

1 **Can you figure out what these floors are?**
   a **im ersten Stock** *on the _____ floor*
   b **im zweiten Stock** *on the _____ floor*
   c **im dritten Stock** *on the _____ floor*
   d **im achten Stock** *on the _____ floor*
   e **im Untergeschoß** *in the _____ floor*

Reading for gist: You don't have to be able to understand every word to find out what floor the facilities are on but you will probably be surprised at just how much you can understand or figure out.

'City Hotel'

Ausstattung

Der Empfang ist im ersten Stock.

Es gibt zwei Bars, Citybar im Erdgeschoß und Discobar im zehnten Stock.

Das Restaurant ist im Erdgeschoß.

Das Frühstücksbüfett befindet sich im zweiten Stock.

Innenpool, Fitnessstudio, Whirlpool, Sauna und Fitnessmöglichkeiten befinden sich im neunten Stock.

Das Wellnesscenter im fünften Stock bietet Friseursalon, Massage- und Schönheitsbehandlungen an.

Das Businesscenter (rund um die Uhr geöffnet), Konferenzraum und Büroservice befinden sich im dritten Stock.

2 **On what floor would you find ...?**
   a Reception   b Breakfast buffet   c Restaurant
   d Citybar   e Fitness centre   f Hairdresser
   g Business centre

3 **Word building. These are all items that are on offer in the rooms in 'City Hotel'. Try to figure out what they are and match them up.**

Es gibt:
   a eine MP3-Dockingstation   i   laundry and cleaning
   b einen Kosmetikspiegel   ii   hairdryer
   c einen Bademantel   iii non-allergic bedding
   d Hausschuhe   iv   slippers
   e einen Fön   v   MP3 docking station
   f einen Kaffee-/Teekocher   vi   bath robe
   g eine Reinigungsservice   vii cosmetic mirror
   h Allergikerbettwäsche   viii tea and coffee maker

4 You want to book a room at 'City Hotel' online.

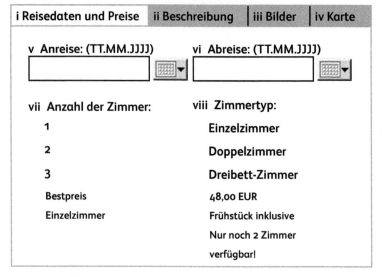

| i Reisedaten und Preise | ii Beschreibung | iii Bilder | iv Karte |

v Anreise: (TT.MM.JJJJ)   **vi Abreise: (TT.MM.JJJJ)**

vii Anzahl der Zimmer: **viii Zimmertyp:**

1   Einzelzimmer

2   Doppelzimmer

3   Dreibett-Zimmer

Bestpreis   48,00 EUR

Einzelzimmer   Frühstück inklusive

                                 Nur noch 2 Zimmer

                                 verfügbar!

Which would you click on:
  a to see a map
  b to key in your arrival date
  c to say how many rooms you want
  d to key in your departure date
  e to say what type of room you want.

5 Write a message to a friend telling him what there is and isn't at this hotel.

Test yourself

 1 Look at Thorsten's form and use it as a model to fill one in for yourself.

Name		Vorname	
Wohnort		Postleitzahl	
Geburtsdatum		Geburtsort	
Nationalität			
Unterschrift			
Handynummer			
E-Mail Adresse			

Name	Müller	Vorname	Thorsten
Wohnort	München	Postleitzahl	74320
Geburtsdatum	05.09.1998	Geburtsort	Frankfurt
Nationalität	Deutsch		
Unterschrift	T. Müller		
Handynummer	0 2 3 4 9 8 7		
E-Mail Adresse	t.muller@hf.de		

2 Now prepare what you would say to give someone the same information over the phone!

SELF CHECK

I CAN...

○	...book a room in a hotel
○	...give personal details
○	...spell my name
○	...ask about facilities
○	...say 'not a'

R2 Review: Units 4–6

1 My family. Fill in the missing word.

a meine _____ my family

b mein _____ my father

c _____ Mutter my _____

d meine _____ my parents

e mein _____ my brother

f _____ Schwester my _____

g mein _____ my son

h _____ Tochter my _____

i meine _____ my children

j mein _____ my husband

k meine _____ my wife

2 a The word for 'my' with masculine words is _____

b The word for 'my' with feminine and plural words is _____

3 Describing people: Read the English and fill in the word missing in the translation.

a *My son is too loud.*   Mein Sohn ist _____ laut.

b *My daughter is quite tall.*   Meine Tochter ist _____ groß.

c *My friend is very small.*   Mein Freund ist _____ klein.

d *He is smaller than me.*   Er ist _____ als ich.

e *My sister is taller than me.* Meine Schwester ist _____ als ich.

f *She is older than me.*   Sie ist _____ als ich.

g *My brother is younger than me.* Mein Bruder ist _____ als ich.

4 Read the text and find the German for the words below:

Mein Freund ist mittelgroß. Er hat kurze blonde Haare und blaue Augen.

Er ist gutaussehend und sportlich. Meine Freundin ist sehr ruhig. Sie ist hübsch und fleißig.

a average size   b short   c hair   d good-looking

e quiet   f pretty   g eyes

5 Translate into German

  a I am average size and I have short brown hair and blue eyes.

  b My friend (m) is bigger than me and he has short dark hair and brown eyes.

  c My friend (f) is shorter than me and she has long blonde hair and grey-blue eyes.

Now write what you are actually like using ich bin and ich habe:

_____

_____

6 Write your own grammar.

In German, nouns are all m _____ , f _____ or n _____

The word for 'the' is

(m) nouns _____ (f) nouns _____ (n) nouns _____

7 Put (m), (f) or (n) after these nouns and write the English meaning

  a der Bahnhof _____   _____

  b die Straße _____   _____

  c das Krankenhaus _____   _____

  d das Kino _____   _____

  e der Flughafen _____   _____

  f die Messe _____   _____

8 Match the German and the English.

  a Wo ist das Hotel?   **i** *Where is the bus stop?*

  b Ist es weit von hier?   **ii** *How do I get to the ariport?*

  c Wie komme ich zum Flughafen?   **iii** *How often does the bus go?*

  d Wo ist die Haltestelle?   **iv** *Where is the hotel?*

  e Wie oft fährt der Bus?   **v** *Is it far from here?*

9 There are two verbs 'to go'.

  a You use _____ when you go on foot.

  b You use _____ when you go with transport.

10 Fill in the correct part of gehen.

  a Wohin _____ du? *Where are you going?*

  b Ich _____ in die Stadt. *I am going to town.*

  c Thorsten _____ zur Messe. *Thorsten is going to the trade fair.*

  d Herr Schuhmacher und Frau Schuhmacher _____ zum Konzert.

  e Wir _____ zum Marktplatz.

  f Wohin _____ Sie?

11 Complete the directions to the station.

Zum Bahnhof? Sie gehen **(a)** _____ *(right)*. und nehmen die
zweite Straße **(b)** _____ *(left)* über die **(c)** _____ *(bridge)* und
immer **(d)** _____ *(straight ahead)*. Der Bahnhof ist auf der **(e)**
_____ *(right)* Seite. Es ist nicht **(f)** _____ *(far)*.

12 Im Hotel. Match the German and the English.

a	ein Einzelzimmer	**i**	*the entrance*
b	ein Doppelzimmer	**ii**	*the emergency exit*
c	ein Zimmer mit Dusche	**iii**	*the lift*
d	der Eingang	**iv**	*the stairs*
e	der Notausgang	**v**	*a single room*
f	der Fahrstuhl	**vi**	*a room with shower*
g	die Treppe	**vii**	*a double room*

13 Match the German and English questions.

a	Haben Sie ein Zimmer frei?	**i**	*How many people?*
b	Wie viele Personen?	**ii**	*How long are you staying?*
c	Wie lange bleiben Sie?	**iii**	*Have you got internet access?*
d	Haben Sie einen Fitnessraum?	**iv**	*There is no reception.*
e	Gibt es Internetanschluss?	**v**	*Have you got a room?*
f	Es gibt keine Funkverbindung.	**vi**	*Have you got a gym?*

14 Write your own grammar.

a to ask '*have you got*' you use: **H** _____ _____?

b to ask '*is there a*' you use: **G** _____ _____?

15 The special word for '*not a*' or '*not any*' is...

a *I haven't got any money:* Ich habe _____ Geld.

b *There isn't a lift:* Es gibt _____ Fahrstuhl.

c *We haven't got a single room:* Wir haben _____ Einzelzimmer.

16 Match the English and the German.

a	Name	**i**	*place of birth*
b	Vorname	**ii**	*family name*
c	Wohnort	**iii**	*post code*
d	Postleitzahl	**iv**	*mobile number*
e	Geburtsort	**v**	*signature*
f	Nationalität	**vi**	*domicile*
g	Unterschrift	**vii**	*nationality*
h	Handynummer	**viii**	*first name*

17 **Do you remember how to say these? Match with the correct German phrase.**

a Good day
b My name
c What's your name?
d How are you?
e Pleased to meet you.
f Do you speak English?
g I don't understand.
h Pardon?
i Please.
j Thank you.
k Would you like a coffee?
l Goodbye.

i Bitte. ii Wie heißen Sie? iii Wie bitte? iv Trinken Sie einen Kaffee? v Wie geht's? vi Auf Wiedersehen. vii Ich heiße... viii Guten Tag. ix Ich verstehe nicht. x Angenehm. xi Danke. xii Sprechen Sie Englisch?

7 Essen
Food

In this unit, you will learn how to:
▶ *say you are hungry and thirsty.*
▶ *recognize some popular German dishes.*
▶ *express preferences.*
▶ *order a meal.*

CEFR: (A1) *Can get an idea of the content of simpler informational material and short simple descriptions (such as menus), ask people for things and handle costs.*

Think of German food – think of Wurst!

Germany is famous for its large variety of **Wurste** (*sausages*) which come in all shapes and sizes. Most sausages contain a large proportion of **Fleisch** (*meat*), **Schweinefleisch** (*pork*), **Rindfleisch** (*beef*) or **Kalbfleisch** (*veal*) but you can also get **vegetarische Wurste** (*vegetarian sausages*).

You can have **Bratwurst** (*roast sausage*) or **gegrillte Wurst** (*grilled sausage*), **Bockwurst** (steamed sausage/Frankfurter), or **Weißwurst** (*white sausages made with veal and bacon and herbs*). These are usually eaten with **Brot** (*bread*) or a bread bun (**Brötchen**), **eine Portion Pommes** (*a serving of chips*), **Senf** (*mustard*), **Ketchup or Mayo** (*mayonnaise*) or **rot-weiß** (*red/white* – with both mayo and ketchup).

Over the 16 days of the Oktoberfest in **München** (*Munich*), 200,000 **Wurstpaare** (*pairs of sausages*), half a million **gebratene Hähnchen** (*roast chickens*), and four million litres of **Bier** (*beer*) are consumed!

> Some words look like English words but don't have the meaning you expect. They are usually called *false friends*. In German, if someone offers you **Peperoni** they are actually offering you jalapeño peppers!

How would you ask for:
sausages _____
mustard _____
a bread bun _____
a portion of chips _____

Vocabulary builder

07.01 Look at the words and phrases and complete the missing English expressions.

FOOD AND EATING OUT!

die Speisekarte	*the menu*
die Getränkekarte	_____
die Weinkarte	_____
die Vorspeise	*starter*
das Hauptgericht	*main course*
die Nachspeise	_____
die Suppe	*soup*
Spargelcrèmesuppe	*cream of asparagus soup*
Fleisch	*meat*
Geflügel	*poultry*
Aufschnitt	*sliced cold meat*
Fisch	_____
Lachs	*salmon*
Gemüse	*vegetables*
Kartoffeln	*potatoes*
Erbsen	*peas*
Bohnen	*beans*
Kohl	*cabbage*
Zwiebeln	*onions*
Knoblauch	*garlic*
Obst	*fruit*
Erdbeere	*strawberries*
Pfirsiche	*peaches*
Kirschen	*cherries*
Salat	*lettuce*
Tomatensalat	*tomato salad*

NEW EXPRESSIONS

Ich esse gern	*I like*
Ich esse nicht gern	*I don't like*
Ich esse lieber	*I prefer*
Ich mag Pasta.	*I like pasta.*
Ich mag kein Pasta.	*I don't like pasta.*
Wie wäre es mit (Schnitzel)?	*What about (Schnitzel)?*

Conversation

07.02 *John has gone to a restaurant for lunch. Listen and follow the text. Then answer the question.*

1 What does he choose for dessert?

John	Ist hier noch frei bitte?
Kellner	Der Tisch in der Ecke ist frei.
John	Die Speisekarte bitte.
Kellner	Bitte schön.
John	Was können Sie empfehlen?
Kellner	Das Schweinefilet mit Champignonrahmsauce und hausgemachten Nudeln?
John	Das klingt gut... ich nehme es.
Kellner	Und als Vorspeise?
John	Was gibt es heute als Tagessuppe?
Kellner	Italienische Gemüsesuppe.
John	ähm .... Das schmeckt mir nicht.
Kellner	Wie wäre es mit einem grünen Salat?
John	Gut, ich nehme es, also ein Salat und das Schweinefilet.
Kellner	Und als Nachtisch? Wir haben heute Käsekuchen, Apfelstrudel, oder Eissorten.
John	Apfelstrudel.
Kellner	Mit Sahne?
John	ähm ... Nein, danke, ohne Sahne.
Kellner	Was trinken Sie?
John	Ein Glas Hauswein.
Kellner	Rot oder weiß?
John	Rot, und... ein Glas Mineralwasser.
Kellner	Kommt gleich.

 07.03 Now listen again and speak John's part.

2 Match the English and the German.

a *What do you recommend?*   i Wie ware es mit...?
b *That sounds good.*   ii Ich nehme es.
c *I'll take it.*   iii Und als Nachtisch?
d *I don't like that.*   iv Das klingt gut.
e *What about...?*   v Das schmeckt mir nicht.
f *And as dessert?*   vi Was können Sie empfehlen?

3 Match the questions and the answers.

a   Ist hier noch frei bitte?

b   Was können Sie empfehlen?

c   Wie wäre es mit einem Salat?

d   Und als Nachtisch?

e   Was trinken Sie?

i   Apfelstrudel.

ii   Gut, ich nehme es.

iii   Der Tisch in der Ecke ist frei.

iv   Ein Glas Hauswein.

v   Das Schweinefilet.

4 Read the conversation again. Are the following statements true (T) or false (F)?

a   John has pork fillet and mushroom sauce as main course.

b   He doesn't like salad.

c   For dessert he orders cheesecake.

d   He has his dessert without cream.

e   For a drink he has a glass of red wine.

Language discovery

1 Find and write the German for the words in bold.

a   The table **in the corner** is free. _____.

b   What can you **recommend**? _____.

c   That **sounds** good. _____.

d   **I'll take** it. _____.

e   What is the **soup of the day**? _____.

f   A glass of **house wine**. _____.

g   Coming **immediately** (straight away) _____.

Learn more

In German, you say:

Ich habe Hunger. *I'm hungry.*

Haben Sie Hunger? *Are you hungry?*

Ich habe einen großen Hunger. *I'm very hungry.*

Ich habe keinen großen Hunger. *I'm not very hungry.*

Ich habe einen kleinen Hunger. *I'm a little hungry.*

Er hat Durst. *He's thirsty.*

> **FALSE FRIEND:**
> **Ich bin voll** means *I am drunk!* I'm full is **Ich bin satt** (*I am satisfied*).

haben _to have_	
sing	plural
ich habe – _I have_	**wir haben** – _we have_
du hast – _you have_	**ihr habt** – _you have_
er/sie/es hat – _he/she/it has_	**sie haben** – _they have_
Sie haben – _you have (polite)_	

WORD BUILDING

Word building is really useful when you are talking about food. When you see very long words on a menu, try to break them up into recognizable parts:

Champignonrahmsauce = **Champignon** + **Rahm** + **Sauce** = _mushroom cream sauce_

hausgemacht = **Haus** + **gemacht** = _home-made_

Tagessuppe = **Tag** + **Suppe** = _soup of the day_

Spargelcrèmesuppe = **Spargel** + **crème** + **suppe** = _cream of asparagus soup_

 PRACTICE

1 Put in the missing part of the verb haben and then match the sentence to the meaning:

  a Ich _____ keinen großen Hunger.   **i** _Are you hungry?_

  b Wir _____ Durst.   **ii** _Are you thirsty?_

  c _____ du Hunger?   **iii** _He's thirsty._

  d Er _____ Durst.   **iv** _I'm not very hungry._

  e _____ Sie Durst?   **v** _We're thirsty._

2 See if you can match the German to the English without looking them up. Do the ones you know first and see if you can work the others out by elimination.

  a die Speisekarte   **i** _soup of the day_

  b das Erdbeereis   **ii** _dish of the day_

  c das Tagesgericht   **iii** _herbal tea_

  d die Tagessuppe   **iv** _main course_

  e die Fleischgerichte   **v** _the menu_

  f die Fischgerichte   **vi** _strawberry ice cream_

  g die Käseplatte   **vii** _meat dishes_

  h das Hauptgericht   **viii** _drinks list_

  i der Kräutertee   **ix** _fish dishes_

  j die Getränkekarte   **x** _plate of cheeses_

Now cover up the German and see if you say them without looking at the conversation.

Listen and learn

07.04 The letters s and z

Listen and repeat. The letter s is pronounced in different ways in German:

s as in **Senf** – *mustard*; **Sahne** – *cream*

s as in **Speisekarte** – *menu*; **Spargelcrèmesuppe** – *cream of asparagus soup*; **Spaghetti**

s as in **süß** – *sweet*; **Süßstoff** – *sweetener*; **Süßigkeiten** – *sweets*; **Weißbrot** – *white bread*

s as in **Schnitzel** – *veal filet*; **Schlagsahne** – *whipped cream*; **Schokolade** – *chocolate*; **Schwarzbrot** – *black bread*

z is pronounced **'ts'** as in **zu** – *to, too*; **Zwiebeln** – *onions*; **Zimt** – *cinnamon*; **Schnitzel**; **schwarz** – *black*

GUTEN TAG...

Vorspeise
a   Tagessuppe
b   Aufschnittplatte
c   Salat

Hauptgericht
d   Schnitzel
e   Hähnchen
f   Fisch
g   Gemüselasagne
h   mit Pommes
i   mit Reis
j   mit Nudeln

Nachtisch
k Apfelstrudel
l Käsekuchen
m Hausgemachten Sorbets

Getränke
n Rotwein
o Weißwein
p Mineralwasser
q Sprudel

 1 07.05 What do they order? Listen and write the letters.

	starter	main course	side dish	dessert	drink
1					
2					
3					
4					

 2 Prepare what you would say to order a meal for yourself.

Write down what you would order and then practise saying it out loud:

Als Vorspeise. Ich nehme _____.

Als Hauptgericht. Ich nehme _____.

mit _____.

Als Nachtisch. Ich nehme _____.

Und zu trinken. Ich nehme _____.

3 And now order for a friend:

Für meinen Freund/meine Freundin

als Vorspeise _____

als Hauptgericht _____

mit _____

als Nachtisch, _____

und zu trinken _____.

Conversation

 07.06 *Thorsten and Jane are in the bar discussing their plans for the evening. Listen and follow the text. Then choose the correct answer.*

Thorsten	Hast du Hunger?
Jane	Keinen großen Hunger.
Thorsten	Hast du Durst?
Jane	Ja... ein Glas Weißwein wäre schön.
Thorsten	Chips oder Nüsse?
Jane	Gibt es Oliven?
Thorsten	Ja, bitte schön. Ein Weißwein für dich und ein Bier für mich. Also isst du gern italienisch, oder ... ähm .... chinesisch?
Jane	Mmm ... ich weiß nicht. Gibt es ein thailändisches Restaurant?
Thorsten	Oder wir könnten was deutsches essen?
Jane	Nein, ich habe Schnitzel zu Mittag gegessen. Ich bin noch satt.
Thorsten	Ich habe nur ein paar Würstchen gegessen. Isst du gern grünen Salat?
Jane	Klingt gut!
Thorsten	Dann gehen wir in die Pizzeria. Ich esse Pizza und du isst Salat!
Jane	Ich mag Pizza auch, aber sie sind so groß und ich bin müde.
Thorsten	OK. Wir bestellen Pizza und einen Salat zum Mitnehmen, und ich hole auch einen DVD.
Jane	Gute Idee.
Thorsten	Was siehst du gern?
Jane	Einen Krimi oder eine Komödie.
Thorsten	Gut, ich auch.

1 **What do they decide to do?**
   a go to the pizzeria   **b** have a typical German meal
   c get a takeaway

07.07 Listen again and speak Jane's part.

2 **Review the expressions below from the conversation. Then match them to the English meaning.**
   a Chips oder Nüsse?   **i** *A takeaway pizza.*
   b Isst du gern italienisch?   **ii** *Do you like salad?*
   c Ich bin noch satt.   **iii** *Sounds good!*
   d Isst du gern grünen Salat? **iv** *Do you like Italian food?*
   e Klingt gut!   **v** *Crisps or nuts?*
   f Pizza... zum Mitnehmen.   **vi** *I'm tired.*
   g Ich bin müde.   **vii** *I'm still full.*

3 **Which of the answers below is correct?**
   a Thorsten has
      i a beer ☐
      ii a glass of white wine ☐
   b Jane only wants a salad because
      i she doesn't like pizza ☐
      ii she is full ☐
   c They decide to
      i go to a pizzeria ☐
      ii have a takeaway ☐
   d They will
      i watch a DVD ☐
      ii go to the cinema ☐

Learn more

The easiest way to say you like something is to add **gern** after the verb.
You can also use **mag** which comes from the verb **mögen** – to like.

You already know **Ich möchte** – *I would like* which is also part of the verb **mögen**.

Liking...

Ich esse gern Pizza.

Ich mag Schnitzel.

and disliking

Ich esse nicht gern Leberknödel.

Ich mag keinen Sauerkraut.

After **mag**, **kein** changes to agree with the noun.

Ich mag keine (Pizza) + **die** *words (fem and plural nouns).*

Ich mag kein (Brot) + **das** *words (neuter nouns).*

Ich mag keinen (Schnitzel) + **der** *words (masculine nouns).*

Does it matter if I get it wrong? Not a lot – the **kein** is the important part and you can always shake your head. Remember the words you say are only part of a conversation. Your tone of voice, facial expression and body language also play a large part!

Singular		Plural	
mögen	*to like*	**wir mögen**	*we like*
ich mag	*I like*	**ihr mögt**	*you like*
du magst	*you like*	**sie mögen**	*they like*
er/sie mag	*he/she likes*		
Sie mögen	*you like (polite)*		

Ich möchte – *I would like*

And preferring:

Ich esse lieber Wiener Schnitzel. – *I prefer Wiener Schnitzel.*

And best of all:

Mein Lieblingsessen ist Brathahn mit Pommes! – *My favourite is roast chicken and chips.*

PRACTICE

1 07.08 **Listen. How do they answer the question: Isst du gern Hähnchen mit Pommes?**

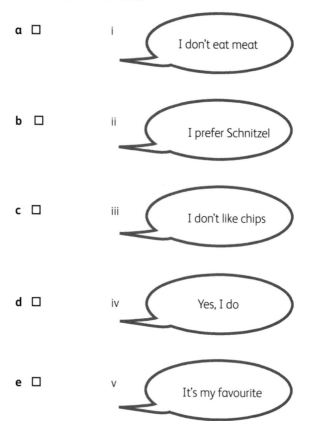

a ☐   i — I don't eat meat

b ☐   ii — I prefer Schnitzel

c ☐   iii — I don't like chips

d ☐   iv — Yes, I do

e ☐   v — It's my favourite

Now you answer the question:

Isst du gern Hähnchen mit Pommes?

2 Complete these sentences with items of your own choice.

Ich esse gern _____

Ich trinke gern _____

Ich mag _____

Ich mag kein[e/en] _____

Reading and writing

1 **Read the breakfast menu below. Can you figure out the words for:**

a hard-boiled egg _____
b scrambled eggs _____
c poached eggs _____
d bacon _____

e potato waffles _____
f pancakes _____
g maple syrup _____
h almond croissant _____

Frühstücks-Menü

Orangensaft oder Grapefruitsaft

Cornflakes oder Müesli

Joghurt

Hartgekochtes Ei, pochierte Eier oder Rühreier

Aufschnittplatte, Käse

Kartoffelwaffeln (mit Ei, Käse, Speck, Schinken, Pilzen und Tomaten)

Pfannkuchen (mit Fruchtkompott und Ahornsirup)

Brot Roggenbrot Knäckebrot Vollkornbrot Brötchen

Croissant, Schokoladen- oder Mandelcroissant

Tee Kaffee oder heiße Schokolade

---

2 Read what Anke says she has for breakfast. See if you can figure out what 'igitt' means:

a Delicious!

b Yuk!

c My favourite!

An den Wochentagen essen wir ein schnelles Frühstück, z.B. Müsli oder Cornflakes mit Milch oder Joghurt, und Vollkorn- oder Roggenbrot mit Schinken und Käse. Normalerweise trinken wir Orangensaft oder Kaffee. Am Samstag essen wir oft Ruhreier oder Omelette mit Schinken und Pilzen aber am Sonntag mache ich meistens Pfannkuchen mit Waldbeeren, Schlagsahne oder Quark (weicher Käse) und Ahornsirup oder Honig. Die Kinder essen die Pfannkuchen mit Nutella (igitt!). Was isst man zum Frühstück, wo du wohnst? Anke

3 Now use Anke's email as a model to write a reply. Tell her what you usually have for breakfast. See if you can include some of the time expressions she uses.

an den Wochentagen – *On weekdays*

am Samstag/Sonntag/Wochenende

normalerweise/meistens/oft

> Notice that the verb always comes after the time expression.
> **Meistens essen wir...**
> **Normalerweise trinken wir...**
> **Am Samstag mache ich....**

 Test yourself

Answer the following questions:

Guten Abend.

Say good evening and ask if there is a place free.

Ja, dort drüben ist frei. Was trinken Sie?

Say what you would like to drink with your meal.

Was nehmen Sie als Vorspeise?

Ask what the soup of the day is.

Linsensuppe.

You don't fancy lentil soup so ask for something else:

Ja, und als Hauptgericht?

Ask what she recommends.

Ich kann den Wiener Schnitzel empfehlen.

Say you like Schnitzel.

Mit Pommes oder Reis?

Say with chips and green salad.

Und als Nachtisch?

Ask if they have any cheesecake.

Tut mir leid, Käsekuchen ist alle. Wir haben noch Sahnetorte.

Say you don't like it.

Wie wäre es mit Apfelstrudel?

Yes, you like Apfelstrudel.

Ja, mit Eis oder Vanillesoße?

You choose!

SELF CHECK

I CAN...
. . . say I am hungry and thirsty
. . . recognize some popular German dishes
. . . ask for recommendations and make suggestions
. . . say what I like and dislike
. . . express preferences.
. . . order a meal

8 Einkaufen
Shopping

In this unit, you will learn how to:
▶ *ask for something.*
▶ *say what size you are.*
▶ *say what colour something is.*
▶ *ask for something different.*
▶ *form the plural.*

CEFR: (A2) *Can ask about things and make simple transactions in shops.*

 ## Wo kann man hier einkaufen? *Where can you shop here?*

In Germany, you can shop in the **Stadtzentrum** *(town centre)*, though nowadays they are often referred to as **City Center**. There you can **machen Ihre Einkäufe** *(do your shopping)* in the small local **Geschäften** *(shops)* or **in einem großem Kaufhaus** *(a large department store)* such as KaDeWe or Karstadt, where you can buy most things under one roof. They usually also have a **Reisebüro** *(travel agent)*, **Café** *(coffee shop)* and a **Restaurant**, often with **Selbst-Bedienung** *(self-service)*. KaDeWe in Berlin is the biggest department store on mainland Europe; only Harrods in London is bigger. The biggest and cheapest and best-known **Kleidergeschäft** *(clothes shop)* is C&A.

Many people like to go to an out-of-town **Einkaufszentrum** *(outlet)* because of the ease of parking. You will find a lot of English words have crept into the shopping scene, such as *Sale, Shopping, Outlet* and lots of words for clothes and fashion: *Large, Medium, Small, Jeans, Slimfit, Straight Leg, Stretch*. So, don't worry. You will have no problem clothes-shopping in Germany!

> **kaufen** – *to buy*
> **einkaufen** – *to shop*
> **verkaufen** – *to sell*

 What do you think a Verkäufer/Verkäuferin does?

Vocabulary builder

08.01 **Look at the words and phrases and complete the missing English expressions.**

SHOPPING

Kleider	*clothes*
Damenbekleidung	*ladies' clothes*
Herrenbekleidung	....
der Anzug(e)	*suit*
der Schlafanzug(¨e)	....
der Jogginganzug(¨e)	....
der Badeanzug(¨e)	....
der Hosenanzug(¨e)	....
die Hose(n)	*trousers*
die Jeans	....
das Hemd(en)	*shirt*
der Gürtel(-)	*belt*
die Socke(n)	*sock*
der Schuh(-e)	*shoe*
die Bluse(n)	*blouse*
der Rock(¨e)	*skirt*
das Kleid(er)	*dress*
das Abendkleid(er)	*evening dress*
das Sommerkleid(er)	*summer dress*
die Unterwäsche	*underwear*
die Jacke (n)	....
der Mantel(¨)	*coat*
der Schal(s)	*scarf*
die Handschuhe	....

NEW EXPRESSIONS

Haben Sie etwas Kleineres/Größeres/Billigeres?
Have you something smaller/bigger/cheaper?

Ich habe Größe 40.	*I'm a size 40.*
Das passt mir gut.	*It fits me.*
Es steht mir gut.	*It suits me.*

Conversation

 08.02 *John is feeling the cold and needs to buy a jersey. Listen and follow the text. Then answer the question.*

1 What size and colour does he ask for?

Verkäuferin	Kann ich Ihnen helfen?
John	Ja, ich suche einen Pullover.
Verkäuferin	Welche Größe? Medium oder Large?
John	ähm ... groß.
Verkäuferin	Und welche Farbe?
John	Blau, dunkelblau.
Verkäuferin	Aus Wolle oder Baumwolle?
John	Wolle.
Verkäuferin	Dieser Pullover kostet €79,90.
John	Das ist ein bißchen teuer. Haben Sie etwas Billigeres?
Verkäuferin	Dieser Pullover aus Baumwolle kostet €39,90.
John	Darf ich ihn anprobieren?
Verkäuferin	Natürlich... passt er?
John	Er ist ein bißchen zu groß. Haben Sie einen in Medium?
Verkäuferin	Ja. Geht das?
John	Ja, er passt mir gut. Ich nehme ihn.
Verkäuferin	Sonst noch etwas?
John	Nein, danke, das ist alles.
Verkäuferin	Bezahlen Sie an der Kasse.
John	Wo ist die Kasse?
Verkäuferin	Dort drüben.

08.03 **Listen again and speak John's part.**

2 Match the questions and answers.

a Welche Größe?
b Und welche Farbe?
c Darf ich ihn anprobieren?
d Passt er?
e Sonst noch etwas?
f Wo ist die Kasse?

i Nein, danke, das ist alles.
ii Dort drüben.
iii Ja, er passt mir gut.
iv Blau, dunkelblau.
v Large.
vi Natürlich.

3 Match the sentences and the correct meanings.

a Aus Wolle oder Baumwolle?   **i** *May I try it on?*

b Das ist ein bißchen teuer.   **ii** *Pay at the cash desk.*

c Darf ich ihn anprobieren?   **iii** *Wool or cotton?*

d Bezahlen Sie an der Kasse.   **iv** *It's a bit too expensive.*

4 What do you think? Read the conversation and answer the questions below.

a What does John want to buy?

b Who is it for?

c What colour does he want?

d What is wrong with the first one he is offered?

e What else does he buy?

Language discovery

Find the expressions in the conversation which mean:

a It suits me.

b I'll take it.

Learn more

GENDER OF NOUNS

In German, all nouns are masculine, feminine or neuter so you have to use:

er (*he*) **sie** (*she*) and **es** (*it*) when referring to them.

Der Pullover is a masculine word (*he*) so John says:

He suits me. I'll take him.

If he had been talking about **die Jeans** or **die Jacke** he would have said:

She suits me. I'll take her. – **Sie passt mir gut. Ich nehme sie.**

PLURALS OF NOUNS

In English, making plurals of nouns is easy because we usually just add an -s, so we don't have to think about it, but, in German, it is more difficult.

The changes needed to make the plural form are usually shown in brackets after the noun in the vocabulary or in a dictionary, for example:

der Gürtel [-] means there is no change and the plural is the same as the singular

der Mantel [¨] means that you add an Umlaut to form the plural: **zwei Mäntel** – two coats

der Schuh [-e] adds an **-e** to become **die Schuhe**

der Rock [¨e] does both – it adds an Umlaut and an **e** – **die Röcke**.

COLOURS *DIE FARBEN*

Work out what the missing words should be. Which one do you think means '*black*'?

rot – *red*

grün _____

grau _____

braun _____

dunkelblau _____

silber _____

blau _____

gelb – *yellow*

schwarz _____

rosa – *pink*

hellblau – *light blue*

bunt – *colourful/multicoloured*

Colours are adjectives, so they have to agree with the noun that follows:

	masc	fem	neut
Ich habe	einen braunen Gürtel	eine rote Jacke	ein blaues Hemd

ASKING FOR SOMETHING DIFFERENT.

Haben Sie etwas...? *Have you anything.... ?*

Kleineres (*smaller*) **Größeres** (*bigger*) **Billigeres** (*cheaper*)

Haben Sie etwas aus Wolle/Leder? – *Have you anything in wool/leather?*

1 **What are the plurals of these words? Write down their meanings.**

der Anzug (¨e) *die Anzüge suits*

der Badeanzug (¨e)

die Hose (n)

die Badehose (n)

das Hemd (-)

der Gürtel (-)

die Socke (n)

2 **Write down the colour with the correct ending.**

Ich suche ... – *I am looking for ....*

a ein _____ Hemd (weiß)

b einen _____ Anzug (grau)

c einen _____ Rock (rot)

d ein _____ Kleid (blau)

3 08.04 **What are these people asking for? Listen and write the number of the words from the box.**

a ☐   **b** ☐   **c** ☐   **d** ☐   **e** ☐

| i cheaper | ii smaller | iii bigger | iv in wool | v in leather |

4 08.05 **Listen and answer the questions.**

What do they want to buy? What colour are they?

a _____   **b** _____   **c** _____

d _____   **e** _____   **f** _____

5 **Choose one item. How would you answer the questions? Not sure? Listen again!**

Ich suche einen/eine/ein _____

Welche Größe?

_____

Welche Farbe?

_____

Kann ich Ihnen behilflich sein?

Ich suche einen/eine/ein _____

Welche Größe?

_____

Welche Farbe?

_____

Conversation

 08.06 *Thorsten meets up with Jane again. Listen and follow the text. Then choose the correct answer.*

1 What is she shopping for?

   a gloves   **b** a new mobile   **c** a new cable

Thorsten	Hallo! Was machst du?
Jane	Ich gehe einkaufen. Und du?
Thorsten	Nichts. Wo gehst du hin?
Jane	Ich weiß es nicht.
Thorsten	Was brauchst du?
Jane	Ein neues Kabel für mein Handy.
Thorsten	Warum?
Jane	Ich habe meines verloren, und ich muss auch ein Geburtstagsgeschenk für meine Mutti kaufen.
Thorsten	Ich komme mit. Was mag sie gern?
Jane	ähm ... Normalerweise kaufe ich ihr Parfüm aber ich würde ihr gern was anderes schenken.
Thorsten	Wie wäre es mit einem Schal?
Jane	Ja, sie trägt oft einen Schal... und sie hat Taschen auch gern.
Thorsten	Es gibt immer schöne Schals und Taschen im KaDeWe und man kann da auch das Kabel kaufen und eventuell da auch essen.
Jane	Gute Idee.
Thorsten	OK. Los!

08.07 **Listen again and speak Jane's part.**

2 Review the expressions below from the conversation. Then match them with the English meanings.

   a Wo gehst du hin?   **i** *birthday present*
   b Was brauchst du?   **ii** *Why?*
   c Warum?   **iii** *Right, let's go.*
   d Geburtstagsgeschenk   **iv** *Where are you off to?*
   e Sie hat Taschen auch gern.   **v** *What do you need?*
   f OK. Los!   **vi** *She also likes bags.*

Language discovery

False friend! The word **eventuell** does not mean eventually, it means *possibly* or *we could*, and it is used when you are making a suggestion or expressing a possibility.

Can you figure out how to say: *I have lost my cable.* _____.

PRACTICE

1 Look at the website and find the words for:

a basket
b enter
c search
d make

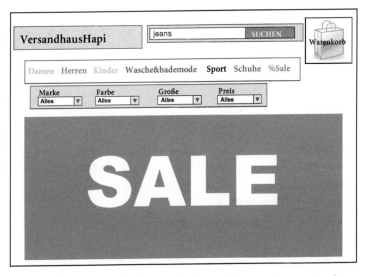

2 Use what you already know to help you figure out new words.

kaufen is the verb to *buy*

ein Kaufhaus is a *department store* or *big shop*.

senden is the verb to *send* or *mail*

a ein Versandhaus _____
b der Katalog _____
c ein Versandhauskatalog _____
d ein OnLine-Geschäft _____

Reading and writing

1 **Read the text below. Find the words for:**

a I wear
b for work
c I have to wear (a suit)
d mostly
e a striped shirt
f from time to time
g or
h in the holidays

Heute trage ich ein weißes Polohemd und Jeans, weiße Socken und weiße Sportschuhe. Für die Arbeit muss ich einen Anzug anziehen. Meistens trage ich   einen grauen Anzug und ein gestreiftes Hemd oder ab und zu ein rosarotes Hemd. Dann muss ich auch normale braune oder schwarze Schuhe anziehen. In den Ferien trage ich am liebsten eine kurze Hose und ein Polohemd.

Thorsten

2 **Using Thorsten's text as a model, write about what you are wearing today, for work and when you are on holiday.**

Remember if you start a sentence with the following words, the verb will follow it.

heute – *today*; **meistens** – *mostly*; **normalerweise** – *normally*; **dann** – *then*

There are two words for to *wear*: **trage – ich trage** – *I wear*; and **ziehen** – *to pull*

*anziehen – *to put on*

*ausziehen – *to take of*

*umziehen – *to get changed*

*These are called separable verbs. You will learn more about them in Unit 9.

Test yourself

Wie kann ich Ihnen helfen?

Say you want a pullover.

Welche Größe?

Tell her your size or say size 40.

Welche Farbe?

Say what colour you would like.

Dieser Pullover ist aus Wolle.

Say it is too small.

Ask if she has something bigger.

Dieser Pullover ist Medium.

Say it (he!) fits you well.

Er kostet €59.

Ask if she has anything cheaper.

Dieser Pullover kostet €39.

Say you'll take it (him!)

Ask where the cash desk is.

Die Kasse ist dort drüben.

SELF CHECK

I CAN. . .
. . . ask for something
. . . say what size I am
. . . say what colour I want
. . . ask for something different
. . . form the plural

Freizeit
Free time

In this unit, you will learn how to:
▶ *talk about hobbies and free-time activities.*
▶ *talk about what you do and when you do it.*
▶ *talk about what you don't do.*
▶ *ask someone what they would like to do.*
▶ *say what you have done.*

CEFR: (A2) *Can describe habits and routines, past activities and personal experiences.*

 Die beliebtesten Sportarten *The most popular sports*

Die beliebteste Sportart *(the favourite type of sport)* in **Deutschland** is **Fußball**. There are more than 6,700,000 **Mitglieder** and about 172,000 **Mannschaften** registered with the **Deutschen Fußballverband** *(German football association)*. **Die Deutsche Fußballnationalmannschaft** *(German national football team)* won the **Fußball-Weltmeisterschaften** in 1974 and 2006.

Other popular sports include **Tennis, Korbball** *(Basketball)*, **Golf, Pferdesport** *(horse-riding)* and **Angeln** *(fishing)* **oder Sportfischen** *(sportfishing)*. Other popular activities include **Schwimmen** *(swimming)*, **Radfahren** *(cycling)* **Wandern** *(hiking)*, **Klettern** *(climbing)* and in Winter, **Skifahren oder Skilaufen** *(skiing)* **Snowboarden** *(snowboarding)*, **Eishockey** *(ice hockey)* and **Rodeln** *(sledging)*.

 Look at the words in bold above. How many of the names for sports can you figure out without looking at the English translation?

DID YOU NOTICE?

Write down how they say:

    a *members* _____
    b *teams* _____
    c *association* _____
    d *world championships* _____

Vocabulary builder

  Look at these words and phrases and complete the missing English expressions.

ZEITANGABEN *EXPRESSIONS OF TIME*

Wann?	*When?*
Morgen	*morning/tomorrow*
Übermorgen	*the day after tomorrow*
Nachmittags	*in the afternoon*
Abends	_____
heute	*today*
heute Morgen	*this morning*
heute Nachmittag	_____
morgen früh	*tomorrow morning (tomorrow early)*
morgen Abend	_____
Übermorgen	*the day after tomorrow*
einmal die Woche	*once a week*
zweimal die Woche	_____
jeden zweiten Tag	*every other day*
montags	*on Mondays*
am Montag	*on Monday*
am Wochenende	*at the weekend*

Remember: If you begin a sentence with a time expression, the verb must come next.

Montags spiele ich Squash. – *I play squash on Mondays.*

NEW EXPRESSIONS

How to ask someone if they would like to do something:

Haben Sie Lust Tennis zu spielen?	*Would you like to play tennis?*
Haben Sie Lust ins Kino zu gehen?	*Would you like to go to the cinema?*
Hast du Lust Karten zu spielen?	*Would you like to play cards?*

> **LANGUAGE TIP**
> The infinitive of the verb is the name of the verb. It is the part you find when you look it up in a dictionary. In English, the infinitive is preceded by *to* (*to play*); in German, it is preceded by **zu** (*to*): **Haben Sie Lust Tennis zu spielen?** – *Would you like to play tennis?*

Conversation

09.02 *Herr Schuhmacher and John run into each other as they are leaving the hotel. Listen and follow the text. Then answer the question.*

1 Where is Herr Schuhmacher going? _____

Herr Schuhmacher	Hallo! Was machen Sie?
John	Ich gehe Joggen. Und Sie?
Herr Schuhmacher	Ich gehe Schwimmen. Ich schwimme zweimal die Woche.
John	Ich gehe jeden Nachmittag joggen.
Herr Schuhmacher	Was machen Sie am Wochenende?
John	Samstag Vormittag gehe ich einkaufen, sonst nichts.
Herr Schuhmacher	Ich habe zwei Eintrittskarten für das Fussballspiel Dortmund gegen Bayern München. Haben Sie Lust mitzukommen?
John	Ja, gerne... Wann beginnt das Spiel?
Herr Schuhmacher	Um 15 Uhr.
John	Wo treffen wir uns?
Herr Schuhmacher	Vor dem Haupteingang, so um 14 Uhr 30.
John	Ja, gut.
Herr Schuhmacher	Und Sonntag Nachmittag hat mein Freund eine Grillparty im Garten. Haben Sie Lust mitzukommen?
John	Ja, schön. Um wie viel Uhr?
Herr Schuhmacher	So um vier. Ich komme vorbei und hole Sie ab.
John	ähm ... Soll ich was mitbringen?
Herr Schuhmacher	Ein Paar Flaschen Bier wäre gut!
John	Gut, ich bringe ein Paar Flaschen mit. Bis dann, Tschüs!
Herr Schuhmacher	Tschüs!

09.03 **Listen again and speak John's part.**

2 What is the correct answer?

    a Where is John going on Saturday morning?
        i jogging   **ii** swimming   **iii** shopping

    b Where is Herr Schuhmacher going on Saturday afternoon?
        i football match   **ii** swimming   **iii** shopping

    c When is the barbecue?
        i today   **ii** on Saturday   **iii** on Sunday

3 Match the questions and answers.

a	Was machen Sie?	**i**	Am Haupteingang.
b	Haben Sie Lust mitzukommen?	**ii**	Um 15 Uhr.
c	Wann beginnt das Spiel?	**iii**	Ja, gerne.
d	Wo treffen wir uns?	**iv**	Ein Paar Flaschen Bier.
e	Soll ich was mitbringen?	**v**	Ich gehe Joggen.

4 Match the English and German.

a	*I have two tickets.*	**i**	Wo treffen wir uns?
b	*When does the game begin?*	**ii**	Ich komme vorbei
c	*In front of the main entrance.*	**iii**	Ich habe zwei Eintrittskarten.
d	*Where shall we meet?*	**iv**	Vor dem Haupteingang.
e	*I'll come by*	**v**	Wann beginnt das Spiel?
f	*and fetch you.*	**vi**	Soll ich was mitbringen?
g	*Should I bring something?*	**vii**	und hole Sie ab.

Language discovery

1 Find the time expressions in the conversation that mean:

  a *twice a week*
  b *every afternoon*
  c *at the weekend*
  d *Saturday morning*
  e *Sunday afternoon*
  f *When*
  g *at about 4*

Now cover up your answers and see if you can say them without looking at the conversation.

Learn more

TALKING ABOUT WHAT YOU DO IN YOUR FREE TIME

You use **gehen** with a sport or pastime where you would use *go* in English.

  Gehen Sie gern tanzen? – *Do you like going dancing?*

  Gehst du gern ins Kino? – *Do you like going to the cinema?*

You use **spielen** with ball games, and card or board games.

  Spielen Sie gern Tennis? – *Do you like playing tennis?*

  Spielst du gern Squash? – *Do you like playing squash?*

REGULAR AND IRREGULAR VERBS

Gehen *(to go)* and **spielen** *(to play)* are regular verbs. They follow the same pattern:

Fahren *(to drive)* is an irregular verb – it does not follow the same pattern.

gehen	spielen	fahren
ich gehe	ich spiele	ich fahre
du gehst	du spielst	du fährst
er/sie geht	er/sie spielt	er/sie fährt
Sie gehen	Sie spielen	Sie fahren

SEPARABLE VERBS

Separable verbs are made up of two words.

i   a prefix, e.g. **ab- an- auf- ein- mit-**

ii a main verb, e.g. **kommen gehen bringen holen**

mit/kommen – *to accompany* **Ich komme mit**. – *I'll come with (you).*

ab/holen – *to fetch* **Ich hole Sie ab**. – *I'll fetch you.*

mit/bringen – *to bring* **Ich bringe eine** – *I'll bring a bottle.*
                    Flasche mit.

PRACTICE

1 **What would you ask Thorsten, if you want to find out if he likes to do the following activities? Use du and gern.**

a go swimming	b play cards	c go jogging	d play football

a _____

b _____

c _____

d _____

2 What would you ask Frau Schuhmacher to find out if she likes to do the following activities? Use **Sie** and **gern**.

a _____

b _____

c _____

d _____

3 Rearrange these words to make sentences. Start with the time expression.

a Woche gehe tanzen die ich Einmal   *I go dancing once a week.*

b ich Jeden joggen gehe Nachmittag   *I go jogging every afternoon.*

c ich Montags um 6 auf Uhr stehe   *On Mondays I get up at 6.*

d ich gehe Morgen Fußballspiel zum   *Tomorrow I am going to a football match.*

e Abend ein Heute in wir Nachtlokal gehen   *This evening we are going to a night club.*

f einkaufen Samstag Am gehe Vormittag ich   *On Saturday morning I am going shopping.*

g Wein mit ich Morgen eine bringe Flasche   *Tomorrow I'll bring a bottle of wine.*

h fliege Nächste ich Woche Amerika nach   *Next week I am flying to America.*

4 Which **Sportart** do they represent? Match the letter of the correct sport to each picture.

| a Fußball | b Radfahren | c Schwimmen | d Segeln |
| e Skifahren | f Tanzen | g Tennis | h Wandern |

i ii iii iv

v vi vii viii

5 09.04 **Listen and complete the chart with the sport they do and when they do it.**

	Activity	When do they do it?
a		
b		
c		
d		
e		
f		

6 **Prepare what you would say to answer these questions about yourself.**

Was spielst du?
Wann oder wie oft spielst du?
Was spielst du sonst gern?
Was spielst du nicht gern?
And what would you say about your friend?
Was spielt deinen Freund/deine Freundin?
Wie oft spielt/macht er/sie das?
Was spielt er/sie nicht gern?

Conversation

 09.05 *Jane and Thorsten have met for a coffee. Listen and follow the text. Then choose the correct answer.*

1 What are they discussing?
  a what they are going to do next   **b** what they like doing
  c their jobs

Thorsten	Morgen Nachmittag habe ich frei. Hast du Lust Tennis zu spielen?
Jane	Leider nicht. Ich mag Tennis nicht.
Thorsten	Spielst du Volleyball?
Jane	Auch nicht!
Thorsten	Schade. Machst du keinen Sport?
Jane	Doch! Ich schwimme, ich fahre Rad, ich gehe gern Wandern, ich gehe jeden zweiten Tag joggen
Thorsten	Fährst du auch Ski?
Jane	Nein, ich fahre nicht Ski...
Thorsten	Was machst du also in deiner Freizeit?
Jane	Ich lese, ich höre Musik, ich sehe ein bißchen fern, ich mache ein bißchen Yoga, ich koche... und du, was machst du?
Thorsten	Im Sommer spiele ich Tennis und fahre Rad und im Winter spiele ich Fussball und am Wochenende fahre ich Ski.
Jane	Ich bin noch nie skigefahren.
Thorsten	Willst du es lernen?
Jane	Gerne!
Thorsten	Und ich habe noch nie Yoga gemacht.
Jane	Willst du es lernen?
Thorsten	Warum nicht?
Jane	Also ich lerne Skifahren und du lernst Yoga... alles klar!
Thorsten	Ich freue mich schon darauf!

09.06 **Listen again and speak Jane's part.**

2 Read the conversation again. Say whether the statements below are T (*true*), F (*false*) or X (*not mentioned*).
  a She doesn't like tennis.   **e** She has never been skiing.
  b She can't play basketball.   **f** He is very sporty.
  c She doesn't like sport.   **g** He doesn't like dancing.
  d She hates jogging.   **h** He has never done yoga.

 Language discovery

Which words from the conversation mean the same as the expressions below?

a Unfortunately
b What a pity!
c Do you also ski?
d What do you do?
e Never
f Why not?
g a bit
h I'm already looking forward to it.

Learn more

1 **Find the expressions in the conversation that mean:**
a I have (never) been skiing. _____
b I have (never) done yoga. _____

So far you have only used the present tense, but if you want to say what you have or haven't done you use the past or perfect tense. In German, the perfect tense is made up of **haben** or **sein** + the past participle.

Ich habe... + past participle.

Ich bin... + past participle.

Most verbs go with **haben** but **gehen, fahren, kommen** and some other verbs of motion go with **sein**.

haben		sein	
ich habe	**wir haben**	**ich bin**	**wir sind**
du hast	**ihr habt**	**du bist**	**ihr seid**
er/sie hat	**sie haben**	**er/sie ist**	**sie sind**
Sie haben		**Sie sind**	

SOME USEFUL PAST PARTICIPLES

machen *to do*: **Ich habe Yoga gemacht** – *I have done yoga*

spielen *to play*: **Ich habe Tennis gespielt** – *I have played tennis*

fahren *to go*: **Ich bin Radgefahren** – *I have been cycling*

gehen *to go*: **Ich bin Schwimmen gegangen** – *I have been swimming*

Remember whenever there are two verbs or parts of verbs in German, you always send the second verb or part of a verb to the end of the sentence.

2 Have you done or not done these things? Answer with a full sentence. Use the table to help you answer the question:

| Ich habe | einmal/zweimal/oft/ noch nie | Tennis/Golf/ Yoga | gespielt gemacht |
| Ich bin | einmal/zweimal/oft/ noch nie | Rad/Ski | gefahren gefahren |

a Haben Sie Tennis gespielt?
b Haben Sie Golf gespielt?
c Sind Sie Radgefahren?
d Bist du Skigefahren?
e Hast du Squash gespielt?

> **LANGUAGE TIP**
> If the question is **Haben Sie** or **Hast du**, your answer starts with **Ich habe**.
> If the question is **Sind Sie** or **Bist du**, the answer begins with **Ich bin**.

 PRACTICE

1 Match the questions and answers.

a Welche Sportarten machst du?
b Wie oft machst du das?
c Was machst du sonst gern? in deiner Freizeit
d Magst du Radfahren?
e Bist du Ski gefahren?
f Was machst du am Wochenende?
g Welche Sportarten machst du nur im Sommer?

i Am Wochenende spiele ich Golf.
ii Ich spiele Squash und gehe Joggen.
iii Im Sommer gehe ich Wandern.
iv Ein oder zweimal die Woche.
v Ich schwimme auch gern.
vi Ich bin noch nie Skigefahren.
vii Ja, ich fahre gern Rad.

Reading and writing

 1 **Thorsten has invited Jane to stay with him and his parents in the Alps. Jane gets this letter from his mother. Read the letter and answer the questions below.**

Liebe Jane

Ich freue mich auf deinen Besuch. Thorsten sagt du machst gern Sport. Er macht auch viel Sport. Er spielt viel Fußball und Tennis. Mein Mann geht jeden Tag Joggen, aber das ist nichts für mich. Ich gehe zweimal die Woche zum Hallenbad schwimmen und Wasseraerobic machen und im Sommer machen wir viele Wanderungen und Radtouren. Im Winter fahren wir gern Ski. Das Skigebiet ist nicht weit von uns, in zehn Minuten sind wir da! Ich mache gern Skialpin aber mein Mann macht lieber Langlauf. Was machst du gern? Wozu hast du Lust, wenn du zu uns kommst? Gehst du auch gern Ski fahren?

Sabine

a Thorsten   b his mother   c his father   d both parents

i   Who likes playing football and tennis? _____
ii   Who goes jogging every day? _____
iii   Who goes swimming? _____
iv   Who goes for walks and bike rides? _____
v   Who likes Alpine skiing? _____
vi   Who prefers cross country? _____

2 **Imagine you are going to stay with Thorsten's family and write a reply as if this letter has been addressed to you, telling Thorsten's mother what you do and what you would like to do when you are there.**

Test yourself

1 Match the expression with the meaning.

a	Morgen	**i**	*on Mondays*
b	Nachmittags	**ii**	*in the afternoon*
c	heute Abend	**iii**	*at the weekend*
d	morgen früh	**iv**	*on Monday*
e	einmal die Woche	**v**	*morning/tomorrow*
f	montags	**vi**	*this evening*
g	Am Montag	**vii**	*tomorrow morning*
h	Am Wochenende	**viii**	*once a week*

2 09.07 Was haben sie am Sonntag gemacht? *What did they do on Sunday?*

	morning	afternoon
a		
b		
c		
d		

3 How would you say the following? Start with the time expressions.

a I go swimming once a week.
b I go jogging every morning.
c I play tennis on Wednesday evening.
d I am playing football tomorrow afternoon.
e I have never been skiing.

SELF CHECK

	I CAN...
○	... talk about hobbies and free-time activities
○	... talk about what I do, and don't do
○	... talk about when I do it
○	... ask someone what they would like to do
○	... say what I have done

10 Eine Reise planen
Planning a journey

In this unit, you will learn how to:
▶ *make travel arrangements.*
▶ *say what you have to do.*
▶ *say what you can do.*
▶ *buy a ticket.*
▶ *use on-line booking.*

CEFR: (A2) *Can get simple information about travel, use of public transport, give directions and buy tickets.*

Visiting Germany

Germany is in the centre of Europe so getting about is easy. Germany has a vey good **Autobahnnetz** *(motorway network)* and a well-developed railway system, **die Deutsche Bundesbahn**, with fast clean **Zügen** (trains) which usually run on time. The fastest train is the **ICE** for which you have to pay **einen Zuschlag** (a supplement).

Getting to Germany: The German national airline is **Lufthansa (LH). Der LH Heimatflughafen** *(the LH home airport)* is in **Frankfurt** but most other large cities, especially **München** and **Berlin**, have **Großflughäfen** *(large international airports)* and frequent **Inland** (national) and **Ausland** *(international)* flights. **Air Berlin** is a budget airline but many other budget airlines also have cheap flights to many German cities. You can book tickets at a **Reisebüro** *(travel agents)* but nowadays most people prefer to **buchen Online** *(book online)*.

Look at the words in bold above. Can you find the German names for:
a   motorway network
b   German railways
c   domestic [flights]
d   international [flights]

Vocabulary builder

10.01 **Look at the words and phrases and complete the missing English expressions.**

Fliegen	*flying*
fliegen	*to fly*
der Flug	_____
der Flughafen	_____
die Flugnummer	_____
der Flugsteig	*the gate*
das Flugzeug	*the aeroplane*
die Abflughalle	_____
Abflüge und Ankünfte	_____
mit dem Zug	*by train*
Abfahrt- und Ankunfstzeiten	*departure and arrival times*
die Abfahrtshalle	_____
ab/fahren	_____
an/kommen	_____
ein/steigen	*to get on (a train/bus, etc.)*
aus/steigen	_____
um/steigen	*to change*

NEW EXPRESSIONS

Wo fährt der Zug nach München ab?	*When does the train to Munich leave?*
Wann komm er in München an?	*When does it arrive in Munich?*
Wo fährt er ab?	*Where does it go from?*
Muss ich umsteigen?	*Do I have to change?*

Conversation

10.02 *John wants to find out about trains. Listen and follow the text.*

1 Where does John want to go?

   a Zug   **b** München   **c** Rückfahrt

> **ab** sounds like *ap*
> **abfahren Abfahrt**
> **Abfahrtshalle**

John	Entschuldigen Sie bitte...
Bahnbeamter	Guten Tag. Wie kann ich Ihnen helfen?
John	Wann fährt der nächste Zug nach München?
Bahnbeamter	Der nächste Zug nach München ist der Intercity. Er fährt um ... ähm ... 11 Uhr 10.
John	Ist der Zug direkt?
Bahnbeamter	Nein, Sie müssen in Mannheim umsteigen.
John	Wann kommt er in München an?
Bahnbeamter	Um 17 Uhr 46.
John	Ich komme Übermorgen zurück. Gibt es einen Zug so um 14 Uhr?
Bahnbeamter	Ja, es gibt einen ICE. ... ähm ... Er fährt um 14 Uhr 35 von München ab. ... ähm ... Er fährt direkt, aber Sie müssen einen Zuschlag bezahlen, oder Sie können mit dem Intercity um 13.05 fahren. Er ist auch direkt. Eine Inter-City Rückfahrkarte ist billiger.
John	Wo kann ich ein Ticket kaufen?
Bahnbeamter	Es gibt einen Automaten dort drüben.
John	Danke ... ähm ... Wo fährt der Zug ab?
Bahnbeamter	Ab Gleis 7.
John	Hat er Verspätung?
Bahnbeamter	Nein, er hat keine Verspätung.
John	Vielen Dank.
Bahnbeamter	Bitte, bitte.

10.03 Listen again and speak John's part.

2 Match the questions and answers.

   a Ist das eine direkte Zugverbindung   **i** Um 17 Uhr 46.

   b Wann kommt er in München an?   **ii** Ab Gleis 7.

                                    iii Er hat keine Verspätung.

   c Wo kann ich ein Ticket kaufen?   **iv** Nein, Sie müssen umsteigen.

   d Wo fährt der Zug ab?   **v** Es gibt einen Automaten.

   e Hat er Verspätung?

3 What do you think? Read the conversation and choose the correct answers.

a When does he want to go?
   i straight away
   ii later today
   iii tomorrow

b When does he want to come back?
   i tomorrow morning
   ii tomorrow afternoon
   iii the next day

c Where does he have to change?
   i München
   ii Mannheim
   iii Übermorgen

d What does he say about the return train?
   i it's cold
   ii it's fast
   iii it's direct

e Where can he buy a ticket? At the:
   i Verspätung
   ii Automaten
   iii Zuschlag

 Language discovery

1 Find the German words in the conversation for the words in bold:

a How **can** I help you?
b **to** Munich
c You've got to **change**
d **at about** midday
e You've got to pay **a supplement**
f **a return ticket** is cheaper
g over **there**
h **It's** not late

Now cover up your answers and see if you can say them without looking at the conversation.

2 Which phrase in the conversation means:

a *You have to*
b *You can*

Learn more

Modal verbs are auxiliary or helper verbs which are used together with another verb. The modal verb *can* is used to convey a possibility; the modal verb *must* is used to convey a necessity.

I can play = possibility

I must play/I've got to play = necessity

Ich kann Tennis spielen. *– I can play tennis (I know how to).*

ich muss Tennis spielen. *– I've got to play tennis.*

müssen		können	
ich muss	**wir müssen**	**ich kann**	**wir können**
du musst	**ihr müsst**	**du kannst**	**ihr könnt**
er/sie muss	**sie müssen**	**er/sie kann**	**sie können**
Sie müssen		**Sie können**	

Remember when there are two verbs you always send the second one to the end of the sentence.

To say *to* with the names of places and countries, you use **nach** (which also means *after* as in **Nachmittag**):

- ▶ with the names of towns, e.g. **nach München** *– to Munich*
- ▶ with countries, e.g. **nach Frankreich** *– to France*
- ▶ and to say you are going home: **ich gehe nach Hause** – I *am going home.*

When you say *to go* (**fahren** and **gehen**), remember to use **fahren** when you use transport:

Ich fahre mit dem Zug/Bus *– I am going by train/bus*

Ich fahre Rad *– I am cycling*

Ich fahre Ski *– I am skiing*

and **gehen** if you go **zu Fuß** *– on foot.*

PRACTICE

1 How would you say:

  a *You've got to change in Mannheim.*
  b *I have to pay a supplement.*
  c *You can change in Köln.*
  d *They've got to go by the Inter-City.*
  e *I can go on the ICE.*
  f *You can change in Köln.*
  g *You can buy a return ticket.*
  h *He can go with the Intercity.*

10.04 **Listen and answer the questions.**

2 a Where is he going?
  b What time is the train?
  c Does he have to change?

3 a Where does she want to go?
  b Which train is recommended?
  c Why?

4 a Where do they want to go?
  b What time is the train they choose?
  c Do they have to change?

5 Fill in your part of the conversation.

Guten Tag. Wie kann ich Ihnen helfen?

Say good day and you have to go to Hamburg.

Wann wollen Sie fahren?

Tomorrow morning

Um wie viel Uhr?

Say about 10.

Es gibt einen Zug um 11 Uhr.

Ask if you have to change.

Nein, der Zug fährt direkt durch.

Ask what time it gets to Hamburg.

Der Zug kommt in Hamburg um 13.25 an.

Say thank you.

Nichts zu danken.

6 Match the signs and their meanings.

a FAHRKARTEN _____

f AUSGANG _____

b ANKUNFT _____

g ZUGFAHRPLAN _____

c HERREN _____

h NOTAUSGANG _____

d ZU DEN GLEISEN _____

i DAMEN _____

e ABFAHRT _____

i arrivals   ii departures   iii to the platforms   iv tickets
v exit   vi timetable   vii ladies   viii gents   ix emergency exit

Conversation

 10.05 Thorsten is coming into the hotel when he meets Jane coming out. Listen and follow the text. The choose the correct answer.

1 Where is Jane going?

    a to the station   **b** to the travel agents   **c** to the airport

Thorsten	Hi! Was machst du?
Jane	Ich gehe zum Reisebüro.
Thorsten	Warum?
Jane	Ich muss meinen Flug buchen.
Thorsten	Hast du noch nicht gebucht?
Jane	Doch, ich habe meinen Flug ab Frankfurt gebucht, aber meinen Anschlußflug nach Frankfurt habe ich noch nicht gebucht.
Thorsten	Also… ich kann das für dich tun… wann fliegst du?
Jane	Warte mal… mein Ticket… so ich fliege um 13 Uhr 20.
Thorsten	Die Flugnummer?
Jane	LH 402.
Thorsten	Ja…
Jane	Was machst du da?
Thorsten	Ich kann den Flug auf meinen Tablet buchen. Ich schaue mal nach … ähm … Es gibt einen Flug… er fliegt um 10 Uhr 10 ab Berlin Tegel… Er kommt in Frankfurt um 11Uhr 25 an.
Jane	Perfekt.
Thorsten	Soll ich den Flug buchen?
Jane	Bitte…
Thorsten	Also Abflughafen Berlin… Zielflughafen… Frankfurt… Rückflug… nein, nur Hinflug… ein Erwachsener LH 181. Gut. Du kannst deine persönlichen Daten selbst eingeben.
Jane	Vielen Dank… Kartennummer… Verfallsdatum… Sicherheits-Code… gut… erledigt.
Thorsten	OK. Ich schicke es dir… und dann hast du dein Ticket auf deinem Handy!
Jane	Hei… das war schnell! Was machen wir jetzt?
Thorsten	Ich hatte eine Idee…
Jane	Ja, sag mal!

10.06 **Listen again and speak Jane's part.**

2 **Review the questions below from the conversation. Then match them to the English meanings.**

a Hast du noch nicht gebucht?

b Wann fliegst du?

c Was machst du da?

d Soll ich den Flug buchen?

e Was machen wir jetzt?

i *When are you flying?*

ii *What shall we do now?*

iii *Should I book the flight?*

iv *Haven't you booked yet?*

v *What are you doing (there)?*

Learn more

Separable verbs are made up of a prefix and the verb. Many verbs can vary their meaning by adding a prefix. You have already seen some of these:

mit – *with*   **mit/kommen** – *to accompany*

Kommen Sie mit? *Are you coming?*

ab – *away*   **ab/fahren** – *to go away/leave/depart*

Wann fahren sie ab? *When are you leaving?*

an – *to*   **an/kommen** – *to come to/to arrive*

Um wie viel Uhr kommst du an? *What time are you arriving?*

PRACTICE

1 **Write down the infinitive of the verb. (The infinitive is the part you would find when you look up a word in a dictionary.)**

a Am Freitag kommt mein Bruder in Berlin an. <u>ankommen</u>

b Er fliegt von Miami am Donnerstag ab. _____

c Er steigt in Frankfurt um. _____

d Seine Frau kommt nicht mit. _____

2 **Rearrange the words to make questions.**

a Sie abfahren wann? *When are you leaving?*

b um Sie in steigen Mannheim? *Do you change in Mannheim?*

c kommen um viel Sie wie Uhr an? *At what time do you get in?*

d Freund mit dein kommt? *Is your friend coming with you?*

3 Thorsten has booked a flight. Look at the webpage and answer the questions below.

  a Where is he going to?
  b Is it for a single or return flight?
  c When is he leaving?
  d Where is he leaving from?
  e When is he coming back?
  f How many people are travelling?

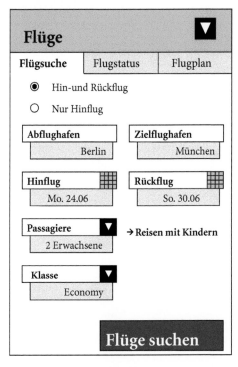

4 10.07 **Thorsten is booking a flight for John. Listen and answer the questions.**

  a Where is he going?
  b Is it for a single or return flight?
  c How many people are travelling?
  d When is he leaving?
  e When is he coming back?

Reading and writing

1 **Jane is sending a message about her flight to her German-speaking agent in America. Read the email and then answer the questions.**

Am Mittwoch fliege ich nach New York. Der Flug von Frankfurt fliegt um 13.20 Uhr ab und ich komme in Newark Flughafen um 15.50 Uhr an. Meine Flugnummer ist LH 402. Der Flug dauert 8 Uhr 30 Stunden und ich würde mich sehr freuen, wenn Sie mich vom Flughafen abholen könnten.

Jane.

   a How long is the flight?
   b What does she say she would particularly like him to do?

2 **Using Jane's writing as a model, write a message to a German friend you are going to visit. Include the following information:**

▶ The number of your flight from London.
▶ What time you are leaving.
▶ What time you arrive in Berlin.
▶ Ask him/her to meet your flight.

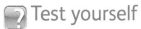

Test yourself

Choose the correct translation:

1	*airport*	**Flughafen**	**Flugplan**	**Flugkarte**
2	*departure*	**Ankunft**	**Abfahrt**	**Abflughalle**
3	*aeroplane*	**Spielzeug**	**Flugzeug**	**Zug**
4	*ticket*	**Frühstück**	**Fahrkarte**	**Flugnummer**
5	*timetable*	**Fahrplan**	**Fahrausweis**	**Reisepass**
6	*to arrive*	**ankommen**	**abfahren**	**anschalten**
7	*to change*	**aussteigen**	**einsteigen**	**umsteigen**
8	*to depart*	**Abfahrt**	**Abfahrten**	**abfahren**
9	*to invite*	**eingeben**	**einziehen**	**einladen**
10	*to have to*	**haben**	**zuhaben**	**müssen**
11	*to be able to*	**müssen**	**können**	**geben**

SELF CHECK

I CAN...
⚪ ... make travel arrangements.
⚪ ... say what I have to do.
⚪ ... say what I can do.
⚪ ... buy a ticket.
⚪ ... use on-line booking.
⚪ ... use separable prefixes.

Congratulations! You have finished the course!

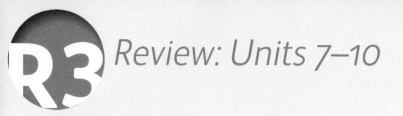

1 Eating out. Match the English and the German.

a	die Speisekarte	**i**	*the main course*
b	die Getränkekarte	**ii**	*the wine list*
c	die Weinkarte	**iii**	*the menu*
d	die Vorspeise	**iv**	*the dessert*
e	das Hauptgericht	**v**	*the drinks menu*
f	die Nachspeise	**vi**	*the starter*

2 Add the missing word to complete the sentences.

a Was _____ Sie empfehlen? *What can you recommend?*

b Das _____ gut. *That sounds good.*

c Ich _____ es. *I'll take it.*

d Was _____ es als Tagessuppe? *What is there as soup of*

e Das _____ mir nicht.   *the day?*

f Wie _____ es mit einem *I don't like it.*
Schnitzel? *What about a schnitzel?*

3 Who likes Schnitzel?

i ***Eva*** Ich mag keinen Schnitzel. Ich bin Vegetarierin.

ii ***Thorsten*** Ich esse gern Zigeunerschnitzel mit Nudeln.

iii ***Stefan*** Ich mag Schnitzel nicht gern. Ich esse lieber Currywurst.

iv ***Sabine*** Schnitzel ist mein Lieblingsgericht, am liebsten esse ich Wiener Schnitzel.

v ***Jörg*** Ich mag Schnitzel mit grünem Salat und Pommes.

a Who likes Schnitzel with salad and chips

b Who likes Wienerschnitzel best?

c Who prefers sausages?

d Who likes Schnitzel with noodles?

e Who doesn't eat meat?

4 **Hungry and thirsty. Put in the correct part of the verb haben.**

Ich _____ Hunger

Mein Freund und ich, wir _____ großen Durst!

Thorsten und Jane _____ Hunger.

_____ du Durst?

Udo _____ keinen Hunger

_____ Sie Hunger?

5 **Clothes! Write in the German word.**

Use the English clue to help you!

a der _____   *coat [mantle]*

b der _____   *scarf [shawl]*

c die _____   *gloves [handshoes]*

d der _____   *belt [girdle]*

e die _____   *trousers [hose]*

f das _____   *dress [clothe[s]]*

6 **Make new words.**

a Winter coat _____

b Leather belt _____

c Wool scarf _____

d Summer dress _____

e tracksuit bottoms _____

f evening dress _____

7 **Word building**

Ziehen is the verb *to pull*. You will see the sign **ZIEHEN** on a door meaning _____

The past participle of 'pulled' is **gezogen**.

A **Zug** is a *train [it is pulled]*.

Anziehen is *to pull on [to get dressed]*.

An **Anzug** is something you pull on [suit].

A **Schlafanzug** is something you pull on to go to bed.

Other **Anzüge** are:

a Jogginganzug _____

b Badeanzug _____

c Hosenanzug _____

Use what you know about prefixes to deduce the meaning of the verbs:

d ausziehen   **e** umziehen

8 When? Match the English and the German.

a	today	i	morgen Nachmittag
b	tomorrow	ii	heute früh
c	this morning	iii	heute Abend
d	tomorrow morning	iv	Übermorgen
e	tomorrow afternoon	v	morgen
f	this evening	vi	heute
g	the day after tomorrow	vii	morgen Vormittag

9 Verbs! Fill in the missing parts of the verb.

A regular verb: **spielen** *to play*

singular		plural	
I play	**ich spiel** _____	*we play*	**wir spiel** _____
you play	**du spiel** _____	*you play*	**ihr spielt**
he/she plays	**er/sie spiel** _____	*they play*	**sie spiel** _____
You [pol] play	**Sie spiel** _____		

Write the grammar rules.

a After **ich** [*I*] the verb ends with _____

b after **du** the verb ends with _____

c after **er/sie/es** [*he/she/it*] the verb ends with _____

d after **wir**, [*we*] **sie** [*they*] and **Sie** [*you polite form*] the verb ends with _____

10 Put the correct part of gehen in the sentence.

a Wir _____ in die Stadt.

b Ich _____ zum Einkaufszentrum.

c Thorsten _____ zum Schwimmbad.

d Sabine _____ zum Reisebüro.

e Jörg und Ilse _____ ins Kino.

f Wohin _____ du?

11 **Fahren is an irregular verb. It takes an Umlaut in the du and er forms. Put the correct form of fahren in these sentences**

a Wir _____ nach Hamburg.

b Ich _____ mit dem Zug.

c Thorsten _____ nach München.

d Sabine _____ nach Italien.

e Jörg und Ilse _____ nach Frankreich.

f Wohin _____ du?

12 Choose the correct word to complete the grammar rule.

When you start a sentence with a time expression the noun/
pronoun/verb has to come next. Begin with the time expression.

Put the words in the right order to make the sentences.

a Schwimmen gehe Einmal   *I go swimming once a week.*
   ich die Woche

b Tennis Mittwochs ich spiele   *I play tennis on Wednesdays.*

c wir Morgen Kino gehen   *We are going to the cinema*
   Abend ins   *tomorrow evening.*

d eine Abend sie gehen   *They are going to a night club on*
   Nachtlokal Freitag in   *Friday evening.*

13 Separable verbs

One verb can have lots of different meanings by simply adding a prefix.
What do these verbs all mean? Match the verb and the meaning.

a	ab/fahren	**i**	*to get off [transport]*
b	an/kommen	**ii**	*to change [clothes]*
c	aus/steigen	**iii**	*to take off [clothes]*
d	um/steigen	**iv**	*to fetch*
e	ein/steigen	**v**	*to get on [transport]*
f	an/ziehen	**vi**	*to arrive*
g	aus/ziehen	**vii**	*to change [transport]*
h	um/ziehen	**viii**	*to put on [clothes]*
i	ab/holen	**ix**	*to depart*

14 Which verb is being used? Use the letters from the exercise above.

i Heute abend hole ich dich vom Hotel ab.

ii Der Zug kommt um 14.30 Uhr an.

iii Morgen fahre ich um halb neun ab.

iv Wir steigen in München um.

v Ich ziehe heute einen Mantel an.

15 Talking about the past. Fill in the missing text.

You use the verb _____ or _____ and the past participle

The past participle usually starts with _____

The past participle always goes to the _____ of the sentences.

Translate the sentences into English

a Am Dienstag habe ich Tennis gespielt.

b Samstag Vormittag sind wir in die Stadt gegangen.

c Am Mittwoch Nachmittag haben wir eine Stadtrundfahrt gemacht.

d Am Sonntag bin ich zum Fernsehturm gegangen.

e Am Freitag ist Jane nach Amerika abgeflogen.

Answer key

Unit 1

North: Nord; South: Süd; European: Europäische

VOCABULARY BUILDER

The missing words are: morning; night

CONVERSATION

1 morning
2 a iii **b** v **c** i **d** vi **e** iv **f** ii
3 a no **b** Udo **c** good **d** good **e** No, unfortunately

LANGUAGE DISCOVERY

1 a Sprechen Sie Englisch? **b** Guten Tag **c** Ich verstehe nicht
d Auf Wiedersehen **e** Angenehm **f** Wie geht's?
2 a Wie heißen Sie? **b** Trinken Sie einen Kaffee?

PRACTICE

1 a -en **b** -en **c** -en **d** -en **e** -en **f** -en
2 a -e **b** -e
3 a Kaffee **b** Restaurant **c** Buch **d** Auto **e** Freund

LISTEN AND LEARN

1 a i **b** 2 **c** 3 **d** 4
2 a ii **b** iii **c** i **d** iv
3 a Tag **b** Sie **c** Name **d** Wie **e** Sprechen **f** danke **g** Trinken **h** Ich
i danke

CONVERSATION

1 a Thorsten München [Süddeutschland] **b** Jane: Manchester [England]
2 a ii **b** vi **c** v **d** i **e** iv **f** iii

LANGUAGE DISCOVERY

1 du **2** du

1 a st **b** st **c** st
2 a Sie **b** du **c** Sie **d** Sie **e** du **f** du
3 a Sie **b** du **c** Sie **d** du **e** du **f** Sie
4 a kommen **b** Sprechen **c** kommst **d** trinken
5 Answers will vary

READING AND WRITING

1 a I am learning **b** Are you learning?
2 a Thorsten **b** München/Munich **c** English

TEST YOURSELF

1 a late afternoon **b** later in the morning **c** early morning **d** night time
2 a formal **b** formal **c** informal **d** informal **e** formal
3 a kommen **b** komme **c** wohnen **d** wohne **e** sprechen **f** kommst **g** wohnst
h sprichst

Unit 2

The words that sound like English words are: **koffeinfrei;
entkoffeinierten; Kaffee; Süßstoff**

VOCABULARY BUILDER

The missing vocabulary is: *a cup of tea; a cup of hot chocolate;* a *glass
[of] wine*

CONVERSATION

1 coffee and chocolate cake
2 a v **b** iv **c** i **d** v **e** vi
3 a black **b** sweetener **c** chocolate cake **d** yes **e** cream

LANGUAGE DISCOVERY

1 a Möchten Sie ein Stück Kuchen? **b** Ja, bitte **c** Ja, gerne! **d** Ich verstehe
nicht **e** Nein danke **f** Geht es? **g** Ohne Sahne **h** Mit Milch.
2 a Haben Sie …? **b** Möchten Sie …?

PRACTICE

1 a v **b** iv **c** ii **d** iii **e** i
2 a Apfelkuchen **b** Käsekuchen **c** Sahnetorte **d** Mineralwasser **e** Rotwein

PRACTICE 2

2 a 7 **b** 3 **c** 10 **d** 0 **e** 6 **f** 4 **g** 11 **h** 20 **i** 8 **j** 1 **k** 17 **l** 5 **m** 2 **n** 19 **o** 12 **p** 18 **q** 14 **r** 16 **s** 1 **t** 15

LISTEN AND LEARN

2 1 h, **2** a, **3** b, **4** d, **5** g, **6** c, **7** e, **8** i, **9** f
4 a 2 **b** 4 **c** 3 **d** 5 **e** 2 **f** 8

CONVERSATION

1 a prosecco and a beer
2 a iv **b** v **c** ii **d** iii **e** i
3 a Schmeckt's? **b** genau richtig

PRACTICE 3

1 a iv **b** iii **c** ii **d** i
2 a ii **b** ii **c** ii **d** i **e** ii **f** i **g** ii
4 €2,20; €5,20; €2,20; €5,20; €4,20; €2,10; €2,10; €2,10; €1,80; €1,80
5 Becher
7 a peppermint tea **b** orange juice **c** green tea **d** camomile tea **e** hot chocolate with cream **f** mug of coffee

READING AND WRITING

1 a orange juice **b** black coffee **c** mineral water **d** decaf with sugar **e** white wine **f** beer and coca cola
2 Answers will vary

TEST YOURSELF

1 a Glas **b** eine Tasse **c** eine Flasche **d** ein Kännchen **e** Dose Cola **f** ein Stück
2 a eine Tasse Tee mit Zitrone **b** ein Glas Rotwein **c** eine Tasse Kaffee mit Milch **d** eine Tasse Kaffee **e** ein Glas Bier **f** ein Glas Weißwein **g** ein Glas Orangensaft

Unit 3

1 um 8 Uhr **2** um halb neun **3** um 6 Uhr **4** um halb eins
What did you notice about the last two answers? In German, instead of saying half past you say half … [to the next hour], and instead of saying a.m. and p.m. they use the 24 hour clock.

VOCABULARY BUILDER

The missing words are: policeman/woman; journalist; student

CONVERSATION

1 Their jobs
2 a iv **b** iii **c** v **d** ii **e** i
3 a F **b** T **c** T **d** F

LANGUAGE DISCOVERY

1 a Freizeitindustrie **b** Finanzberater **c** Sprachkursus **d** Sind Sie verheiratet?
2 a here **b** finance **c** house **d** clinic
3 a Was machen Sie? **b** Was macht sie?
4 a you **b** you **c** she **d** she

LEARN MORE

1 a in einem Büro **b** in einem Krankenhaus **c** in einer Klinik
d in einer Bank
2 a iii **b** i **c** iii

LISTEN AND LEARN

1 1 e, **2** d, **3** b, **4** f, **5** c, **6** a
2 1 c, **2** a, **3** e, **4** d, **5** b
3 a Beruf **b** bin **c** Wo **d** einer **e** Sie **f** Was **g** Sie **h** arbeitet
i einem Krankenhaus **j** er **k** ist; einem
4 Answers will vary

CONVERSATION

1 Jane is a journalist, Thorsten is a Web Designer
2 a iii **b** iv **c** v **d** i **e** ii

PRACTICE

1

Wir treffen uns am Dienstag den 25sten Juli
Wir treffen uns am Mittwoch den 18ten August
Wir treffen uns am Freitag den 31sten Mai
Wir treffen uns am Donnerstag den 15ten Oktober
Wir treffen uns am Sonntag den 29sten September
Wir treffen uns am Samstag den 22sten Januar
Wir treffen uns am Montag den 24sten Marz

2 a Meine Handynummer lautet 0 7 7 4 6 9 3 2 **b** Meine Handynummer lautet 0 4 3 6 7 9 8 5 **c** Meine Handynummer lautet 0 5 2 4 3 6 7 9 8
3 Answers will vary

1 a Jörg **b** Franz **c** Udo **d** Hannelore **e** Elke **f** Uta

1 a Was sind Sie von Beruf? Ich bin Elektriker **b** Wo arbeiten Sie? In einer Automobilfabrik **c** Sind Sie verheiratet? Ja, meine Frau heißt Helga **d** Was macht sie? Sie ist Sekretärin **e** Wo arbeitet sie? In einem Büro
2 Answers will vary
3 a acht Uhr fünfzehn **b** neun Uhr zwanzig **c** zehn Uhr dreißig **d** zwolf Uhr fünfundvierzig **e** vierzehn Uhr zehn **f** siebzehn Uhr fünfundzwanzig **g** achtzehn Uhr fünfundfünfzig **h** neunzehn Uhr

Unit 4

The words are: wedding – **Hochzeit**; married – **verlobt**; engaged – **verheiratet**; separated – **getrennt**; divorced – **geschieden**

The missing words are: my mother; my brother; my son; my daughter; my grandmother; my grandparents

1 They are discussing children
2 a Haben Sie Kinder? **b** noch nicht **c** Wie ist er? **d** zu laut **e** Das wäre nichts für mich! **f** Für mich auch nicht!
3 a iv **b** iii **c** ii **d** i

1 a er ist **b** er spielt **c** er flirtet **d** sie ist **e** sie geht **f** sie studiert
2 a mein **b** meine **c** mein **d** meine **e** meine **f** mein **g** meine **h** meine **i** meine **j** meine **k** mein **l** meine
3 The right words are: **a** masc **b** fem and plural

1 The right word is: **a** he **b** they **c** she **d** they **e** he **f** she

1 a ii **b** iv **c** iii **d** vii **e** vi **f** v **g** i
2 The missing words are: **a** Sohn **b** Frau **c** Tochter **d** Vater **e** Oma
3 a iv **b** iii **c** v **d** vi **e** i **f** ii
4 Answers will vary

CONVERSATION

1 c other people
2 The correct meanings are: **a** ii **b** i **c** ii **d** iii

LANGUAGE DISCOVERY

1 The phrase is: Und hast du noch andere Geschwister?
2 The phrases are: **a** Er ist größer als ich, und dicker **b** Ist er älter oder jünger? **c** Sie ist kleiner als ich

PRACTICE

1 Answers will vary
2 Answers will vary

READING AND WRITING

1 The meaning of the words is: **a** musician **b** engaged **c** wedding
2 a his mother **b** his sister **c** his brother **d** his sister **e** her boyfriend **f** June
3 Answers will vary

TEST YOURSELF

1 The correct words are: **a** average **b** dark hair and brown eyes **c** sporty **d** football **e** married **f** daughter
2 Answers will vary
3 Answers will vary

Unit 5

The features these towns were named after are: castle; bridge; church; mountain

VOCABULARY BUILDER

The missing words are: bank; airport; hotel; information office; cinema; restaurant; main street; theatre

NEW EXPRESSIONS

The missing words are: hotel; bus stop; bus

CONVERSATION

1 a

2 a v **b** i **c** iv **d** iii **e** ii

3 a hotel Europa **b** in the main street **c** no **d** right **e** airport **f** [shuttle]bus

LANGUAGE DISCOVERY

1 a Wie kann ich Ihnen helfen? **b** in der Hauptstraße **c** Ist es weit? **d** Am besten fahren Sie mit dem Bus **e** Sie gehen hier links **f** Er fährt alle 20 Minuten **g** vor dem Hauptbahnhof **h** Nichts zu danken. Gern geschehen.
2 a Sie gehen hier links **b** Sie fahren mit dem Bus

PRACTICE

1 a der mountain **b** die library **c** die bridge **d** die castle **e** der cathedral **f** das shopping centre **g** der river **h** die main city **i** die church **j** die art gallery **k** der market place **l** das museum **m** das town hall **n** das Schloß
2 a Die Hauptstadt **b** der Hauptbahnhof **c** die Hauptstraße
d der Stadtplan **e** das Stadtzentrum
3 a the tram[way] **b** the Underground/Subway **c** the motorway
4 a zum **b** zum **c** zum **d** zum **e** zur **f** zum
The answers were mostly zum

LISTEN AND LEARN

1 a iii **b** v **c** i **d** ii **e** iv
2 a iv **b** v **c** ii **d** iii **e** i

CONVERSATION

1 c
2 a v **b** iv **c** i **d** iii **e** ii
3 a v **b** iii **c** iv **d** ii **e** i

LANGUAGE DISCOVERY

1 Ausfahrt

PRACTICE

2 a an der Ampel rechts **b** über die Brücke **c** Sie gehen/fahren immer geradeaus **d** Sie können es nicht verfehlen **e** die erste Straße links

READING AND WRITING

1 i b **ii** a **iii** e **iv** c **v** d

TEST YOURSELF

1 a der Bahnhof **b** die Bank **c** das Hotel **d** das Krankenhaus

2 a zum Bahnhof **b** zur Bank **c** zum Hotel **d** zum Krankenhaus

3 a iv **b** vi **c** v **d** i **e** ii **f** iii

4 a die Bank **b** die Brücke **c** das Rathaus **d** der Bahnhof **e** das Schloß or die Burg

5 a zum **b** zur **c** zum **d** zum **e** zur

Unit 6

The German word for lunch is **Mittagessen**

VOCABULARY BUILDER

a double room; a room with bath; a room with shower; exit; toilets; receptionist [f]; receptionist [m]

NEW EXPRESSIONS

people; nights; long; fitness; internet

CONVERSATION

1 Two nights

2 a ii **b** v **c** iv **d** i **e** vi **f** iii

3 a No **b** single **c** by car **d** third **e** Sign in

LANGUAGE DISCOVERY

1 a iii **b** iv **c** v **d** ii **f** i **g** vi **h** vii

2 a Wie viel? **b** wie lange?

PRACTICE

1 a Haben Sie Internetanschluss? **b** Gibt es einen Fahrstuhl? **c** Wie viele Personen? **d** Wie lange bleiben Sie? **e** Haben Sie einen Fitnessraum? **f** Gibt es Funkverbindung?

2 a Ich babe keine Schwester **b** Er hat kein Auto **c** Sie hat keinen Bruder **d** Er hat kein Geld **e** Ich habe keine Funkverbindung

3 a Fischer **b** Schneider **c** Hartmann **d** Müller **e** Högemann

4 a Berlin **b** Hamburg **c** Dortmund **d** Regensburg **e** München

5

	type of room	length of stay
a	double	two
b	single	week
c	double	two weeks
d	3 bed	2 nights
e	family room	1 night

6 Guten Abend. Haben Sie ein Zimmer frei? Einzelzimmer/Doppelzimmer. Eine Nacht/zwei Nächte. Wie viel kostet es? Mit Frühstück? Wo kann ich hier parken? Tut mir leid, ich verstehe nicht. Danke schön.

CONVERSATION

1 407; 4th
2 a Wie ist Ihr Name? **b** Und Ihr Vorname? **c** Wie schreibt man das? **d** Wie ist Ihre Adresse? **e** Wie ist die Postleitzahl? **f** Haben Sie eine Handynummer?

LANGUAGE DISCOVERY

1 a Geburtsort **b** Ich muß Ihre Kreditkarte durchziehen.

PRACTICE

1 a first **b** second **c** third **d** eighth **e** basement
2 a 1st **b** 2nd **c** ground floor **d** ground floor **e** 9th **f** 5th **g** 3rd
3 a v **b** vii **c** vi **d** iv **e** ii **f** viii **g** i **h** iii
4 a iv **b** v **c** vii **d** vi **e** viii
5 Answers will vary

TEST YOURSELF

Answers will vary

Unit 7

The missing foods are: **Wurst; Senf; ein Brötchen; eine Portion Pommes**

VOCABULARY BUILDER

drinks list;

VOCABULARY BUILDER

wine list; dessert; fish

CONVERSATION

1 Apfelstrudel
2 a vi **b** iv **c** ii **d** v **e** i **f** iii
3 a iii **b** v **c** ii **d** i **e** iv
4 a T **b** F **c** F **d** F **e** T **f** T

LANGUAGE DISCOVERY

1 a in der Ecke **b** empfehlen **c** klingt **d** ich nehme **e** Tagessuppe
f Hauswein **g** gleich

PRACTICE

1 a habe; iv **b** haben; v **c** hast; ii **d** hat; iii **e** Haben; i
2 a v **b** vi **c** ii **d** i **e** vii **f** ix **g** x **h** iv **i** iii **j** viii

GUTEN TAG

11 a f I k o
2 b d h m q
3 g c l n
4 c e j m p
2 Answers will vary
3 Answers will vary

CONVERSATION

1 c
2 a v **b** iv **c** vii **d** ii **e** iii **f** I **g** vi
3 a i **b** ii **c** ii **d** i

PRACTICE

1 a iv **b** iii **c** i **d** v **e** ii
2 Answers will vary

READING AND WRITING

1 a hartgekochtes Ei **b** Rührreier **c** pochierte Eier **d** Speck **e** Kartoffelwaffeln
f Pfannkuchen **g** Ahornsirup **h** Mandelcroissant
2 b ·
3 Answers will vary

Unit 8

A **Verkäufer/Verkäuferin** is a shop assistant or salesperson

VOCABULARY BUILDER

In order the missing clothing items are: menswear; pyjamas; track suit; swimsuit; trouser suit; jeans; jacket; gloves

CONVERSATION

1 large, dark blue
2 a v **b** iv **c** vi **d** iii **e** i **f** ii
3 a iii **b** iv **c** i **d** ii
4 a a pullover **b** himself **c** dark blue **d** too expensive **e** nothing

LANGUAGE DISCOVERY

It suits me: Sie passt mir gut. I'll take it: Ich nehme sie.
The missing colours are green; grey; brown; dark blue; silver; blue; black

LEARN MORE

green, grey, brown, dark brown, silver, blue, black

PRACTICE

1
der Anzug die Anzüge   suits
der Badeanzug die Badeanzüge   swimming costumes
die Hose die Hosen   trousers
die Badehose die Badehosen   swimming trunks
das Hemd die Hemden   shirts
der Gürtel die Gürtel   belts
die Socke die Socken   socks
2 a weißes **b** grauen **c** roten **d** blaues
3 a iv **b** ii **c** i **d** iii **e** v
4 a white shirt **b** dark grey trousers **c** white trainers **d** dark blue evening dress **e** black coat **f** beige suit
5 Answers will vary

CONVERSATION

1 c **2 a** iv **b** v **c** ii **d** i **e** vi **f** iii

Ich habe mein Kabel verloren.

PRACTICE

1 a Warenkorb **b** eingeben **c** Suchen **d** Mark
2 a mail order company **b** catalogue **c** mail order catalogue **d** on-line shop

READING AND WRITING

1 a ich trage **b** Für die Arbeit **c** muss ich einen Anzug anziehen **d** meistens
e ein gestreiftes Hemd **f** ab und zu **g** oder **h** in den Ferien

TEST YOURSELF

Ich möchte einen Pullover. Größe 40. Blau. Er ist zu klein. Haben Sie etwas Größeres. Er passt mir gut. Haben Sie etwas Billigeres? Ich nehme ihn. Wo ist die Kasse?

Unit 9

a Mitglieder **b** Mannschaften **c** Verband **d** Weltmeisterschaften

VOCABULARY BUILDER

in the evening; this afternoon; tomorrow evening; twice a week

CONVERSATION

1 swimming
2 a i **b** ii **c** iii
3 a v **b** iii **c** ii **d** i **e** iv
4 a iii **b** v **c** iv **d** i **e** ii **f** vii **g** vi

LANGUAGE DISCOVERY

1 a zweimal die Woche **b** jeden Nachmittag **c** am Wochenende
d Samstag Vormittag **e** Sonntag Nachmittag **f** wann **g** so um 16 Uhr

PRACTICE

1 a Gehst du gern Schwimmen? **b** Spielst du gern Karten? **c** Gehst du gern Joggen? **d** Spielst du gern Fußball?
2 a Gehen Sie gern ins Kino? **b** Spielen Sie gern Tennis? **c** Spielen Sie gern Schach? **d** Gehen Sie gern Skifahren?
3 a Einmal die Woche gehe ich tanzen. **b** Jeden Nachmittag gehe ich

joggen. **c** Montags stehe ich um 6 Uhr auf. **d** Morgen gehe ich zum Fußballspiel. **e** Heute Abend gehen wir in ein Nachtlokal. **f** Am Samstag Vormittag gehe ich einkaufen. **g** Morgen bringe ich eine Flasche Wein mit. **h** Nächste Woche fliege ich nach Amerika.

4 i b, **ii** g, **iii** d, **iv** f, **v** h, **vi** a, **vii** c, **viii** e

5 a tennis once a week **b** hiking weekend **c** bike riding Sunday morning **d** football twice a week **e** swimming three times a week **f** dancing on Fridays

6 Answers will vary

1 b

2 a T **b** x **c** F **d** F **e** T **f** T **g** x **h** T

a Leider **b** Schade **c** fährst du auch Ski? **d** also was machst du? **e** noch nie **f** warum nicht? **g** ein bisschen **h** Ich freue mich schon darauf.

1 a Ich bin [noch nie] Skigefahren. **b** Ich habe [noch nie] Yoga gemacht.

1 a ii **b** iv **c** v **d** vii **e** vi **f** i **g** iii

1 i a **ii** c **iii** b **iv** d **v** b **vi** c

2 Answers will vary

1 a v **b** ii **c** vi **d** vii **e** viii **f** i **g** iv **h** iii

2 a swimming; tennis **b** jogging; football **c** cycling; squash **d** skiing; yoga

3 a Einmal die Woche gehe ich schwimmen. **b** Jeden Vormittag gehe ich joggen. **c** Mittwoch Abend spiele ich Tennis. **d** Morgen Nachmittag gehe ich zum Fußballspiel. **e** Samstag gehe ich ins Kino.

Unit 10

a Rhein **b** das Mittelmeer **c** Donau **d** Wien

VOCABULARY BUILDER

The missing words are: flight ; airport ; flight number; departure lounge; departures and arrivals ; departure lounge [train]; to depart to arrive; to get off … to change

1 b
2 a iv b i c v d ii e iii
3 a i b iii c ii d iii e ii

LANGUAGE DISCOVERY

1 a kann b nach c umsteigen d so um e Zuschlag f eine Rückfahrkarte g dort h er
2 a sie müssen b sie können

PRACTICE

1 a Sie müssen in Mannheim umsteigen. b Ich muss einen Zuschlag bezahlen. c Sie können in Köln umsteigen. d Sie müssen mit dem Intercity fahren. e Sie können mit dem Intercity fahren. f Sie können in Köln umsteigen. g Sie können eine Rückfahrkarte kaufen. h Er kann mit dem Intercity fahren.
2 a Hamburg b 14.35 c no
3 a München b Intercity c cheaper
4 a Berlin b 10.45 c no
5 Guten Tag. Ich muss nach Hamburg fahren; Morgen früh; so um 10; Muss ich umsteigen?; Wann kommt er in an?; Vielen Dank
6 a iv b i c viii d iii e ii f v g vi h ix i vii

CONVERSATION

1 b
2 a iv b i c v d iii e ii

PRACTICE

1 a ankommen b abfliegen c umsteigen d mitkommen
2 a Wann fahren Sie ab? b Um wie viel Uhr kommen an? c Steigen Sie in Mannheim um? d Kommt dein Freund mit?
3 a München b return flight c 24 June d Berlin e 30 June f two people
4 a London b return c 1 person d 22nd July e 30 July

READING AND WRITING

1 a eight and half hours b meet her at the airport

1 Flughafen **2** Abfahrt **3** Flugzeug **4** Fahrkarte **5** Fahrplan **6** ankommen
7 umsteigen **8** abfahren **9** einladen **10** müssen **11** können

Review 1

1 b
2 a iv **b** vi **c** vii **d** i **e** iii **f** v **g** ii
3 a Sie **b** du **c** Sie **d** du **e** Sie **f** du
4 a -st **b** -en
5 a ii **b** iii **c** iv **d** i
6 a iv **b** vi **c** v **d** i **e** ii **f** iii
7 gern; lieber **a** gern **b** lieber **c** gern **d** lieber
8 a iii **b** vii **c** iv **d** v **e** vi **f** ii **g** i
9 a Studentin; student **b** Lehrerin; teacher **c** Krankenpflegerin; nurse
  d Journalistin; journalist
10 a Ich bin Manager. Ich arbeite in einem Reisebüro **b** Er ist
Finanzberater. Er arbeitet in einer Bank **c** Sie ist Ärztin. Sie arbeitet in
einem Krankenhaus.

Review 2

1 a Familie **b** Vater **c** meine **d** Eltern **e** Bruder **f** meine **g** Sohn **h** meine
Tochter **i** Kinder **j** Mann **k** Frau
2 a mein **b** meine
3 a zu **b** ganz **c** sehr **d** kleiner **e** größer **f** älter **g** jünger
4 a mittelgroß **b** kurze **c** Haare **d** gutaussehend **e** ruhig **f** hübsch
g Augen
5 a Ich bin mittelgroß und habe kurze braune Haare und blaue Augen.
b Mein Freund is größer als ich und hat kurze dunkle Haare und braune
Augen. **c** Meine Freundin ist kleiner als ich und hat lange blonde Haare
und grau-blaue Augen.
6 masculine, feminine, neuter; der, die, das
7 a station, m **b** street, f **c** hospital, n **d** cinema, n **e** airport, m **f** trade fair, f
8 a iv **b** v **c** ii **d** i **e** iii
9 a gehen **b** fahren
10 a gehst **b** gehe **c** geht **d** gehen **e** gehen **f** gehen
11 a rechts **b** links **c** Brücke **d** geradeaus **e** rechten **f** weit
12 a v **b** vii **c** vi **d** i **e** ii **f** iii **g** iv
13 a v **b** i **c** ii **d** vi **e** iii **f** iv
14 a Haben Sie? **b** Gibt es?

15 a kein **b** keinen **c** kein
16 a ii **b** viii **c** vi **d** iii **e** i **f** vii **g** v **h** iv
17 a viii **b** vii **c** ii **d** v **e** x **f** xii **g** ix **h** iii **i** i **j** xi **k** iv **l** vi

Review 3

1 a iii **b** v **c** ii **d** vi **e** i **f** iv
2 a können **b** klingt **c** nehme **d** gibt **e** schmeckt **f** war
3 a v **b** iii **c** iv **d** ii **e** i
4 a habe **b** haben **c** haben **d** hast **e** hat **f** haben
5 a Mantel **b** Schal **c** Handschuhe **d** Gürtel **e** Hose **f** Kleid
6 a Wintermantel **b** Ledergürtel **c** Wollschal **e** Jogginghose
f Abendkleid
7 a tracksuit **b** swim suit **c** trouser suit **d** undress **e** change
8 a vi **b** v **c** ii **d** vii **e** i **f** iii **g** iv
9 ich spiele; du spielst; er spielt; Sie spielen; wir spielen; sie spielen
10 a gehen **b** gehe **c** geht **d** geht **e** gehen **f** gehst
11 a fahren **b** fahre **c** fährt **d** fährt **e** fahren **f** fährst
12 verb **a** Einmal die Woche gehe ich Schwimmen **b** Mittwochs spiele
ich Tennis **c** Morgen Abend gehen wir ins Kino **d** Freitag Abend gehen
sie in eine Nachtlokal
13 a ix **b** vi **c** i **d** vii **e** v **f** viii **g** iii **h** ii **i** iv
14 i i **ii** ii **iii** a **iv** d **v** f
15 a On Tuesday I played tennis **b** On Saturday morning we went to town
c On Wednesday afternoon we went for a city tour **d** On Sunday I went to
the television tower **e** On Friday Jane flew to America

German–English vocabulary

Abend m *(e)*   *evening*
    abends   *in the evening*
    heute Abend   *this evening*
alt   *old*
    älter   *older*
an   *on,*
    am... *(an + dem)*   *on the*
angenehm   *pleased/it's a pleasure*
an/probieren   *to try (a garment) on*
Anzug m *("e)*   *suit*
auch   *also*
auf   *on:*
    auf der rechten/linken Seite   *on the right/left side*
aus   *from/out of*
Auskunft f *("e)*   *information*
Ausland   m *abroad*
Auto n *(s)*   *car*
    Autobahn   f *motorway*
Bad n   *bath*
Bahnhof m *("e)*   *station*
Berg m   *mountain*
Beruf m *("e)*   *job*
    berufstätig   *employed*
bestellen   *to order*
Bett n *(en)*   *Bed*
    Doppelbett   *double bed*
    Einzelbett   *single bed*
bezahlen   *to pay*
Bibliothek   *library*
billig   *cheap*
    etwas Billigeres   *something cheaper*
bin (ich bin)   *(I) am*
bis   *until*
bißchen   *a bit*

bitte   *please*
    wie bitte?   *pardon?*
    bitte schön   *here you are*
bitte, bitte   *don't mention it*
Brücke f *(n)*   *bridge*
Burg f   *castle*
Büro n *(s)*   *office*
Campingplatz m *("e)*   *campsite*
da   *there*
danke/danke schön   *thank you*
dann   *then*
das tut mir Leid   *I'm sorry*
dort drüben   *over there*
Dose f *(n)*   *tin/can*
    eine Dose Cola   *a can of coke*
du   *you (friendly form)*
    dich   *yourself*
    dir   *(to) you*
drücken   *to press/push/print*
dunkel   *dark*
Durst m   *thirst*
    ich habe Durst   *I'm thirsty*
Dusche f *(n)*   *shower*
Ecke f *(n)*   *corner*
Empfangstisch   m *reception desk*
    Empfangsdame   f *receptionist*
    Empfangsherr   m *receptionist*
entschuldigen Sie, bitte   *excuse me, please*
er   *he*
erst/e   *the first*
    am ersten   *on the first*
es   *it*
    es geht mir gut   *I am well*
essen   *to eat*
etwas   *some*
    sonst noch etwas?   *anything else?*

fahren *to drive*
    ich fahre *I drive*
Fahrstuhl m *lift*
Familie f *(n)* *family*
Farbe f *(n)* *colour*
Fernseher m *television*
    Farbfernseher *colour television*
    fernsehen *to watch television*
Flasche f *(n)* *bottle*
fliegen *to fly*
    Flughafen m *airport*
    Flugzeug n *plane*
Frau f *(en)* *woman/wife/Mrs*
Fräulein n *(-)* *young lady/Miss*
frei *free*
Freibad n *(¨er)* *open-air swimming pool*
freuen *to look forward to*
    ich freue mich… *I am looking forward…*
Frühstück n *breakfast*
für *for*
Fuß m *(¨e)* *foot*
    zu Fuß *on foot*
ganz *quite*
geben *to give*
    es gibt *there is*
Geburt *birth*
    Geburtstag m *birthday*
    Geburtsdatum *date of birth*
gehen *to go*
    ich gehe *I go*
    geht das? *is that all right?*
    es geht *it's all right*
genau *exactly*
geradeaus *straight ahead*
gern/e *willingly/with pleasure*
Geschäft n *(¨e)* *shop business*
Glas n *(¨er)* *glass*
gleich *immediately/straight away*
groß *big*
    größer *bigger*
    etwas Größeres *something bigger*

die Größe f *size*
gucken *to look*
gut *good/well*
haben *to have,*
    ich habe *I have*
haben Sie…? *have you…?*
halb *half*
    halbtrocken *half dry/medium dry*
Handy n *mobile phone*
haupt *main*
    Hauptbahnhof m *main station*
    Hauptstadt f *main town/ capital city*
heiß *hot*
heißen *to be called*
    ich heiße *I am called*
der Herr m *(en)* *man/Mr/husband*
heute
hier *here*
hinter *behind*
holen *to fetch*
    ich hole *I fetch*
    abholen *to fetch/ pick up*
Hunger m *hunger*
    ich habe Hunger *I'm hungry*
ich *I*
immer *always*
inbegriffen *included*
ja *yes*
kalt *cold*
kaufen *to buy*
    ich kaufe *I buy*
    einkaufen *to shop*
    verkaufen *to sell*
kein/e *not a*
    ich habe kein/e/en… *I haven't a…*
Kännchen n *small can/pot*
Kino n *cinema*
Kirche f *church*
klein *small*
    kleiner *smaller*
    etwas Kleineres *something smaller*

kommen *to come*
    ich komme *I come*
    an/kommen *to arrive*
    vorbei/kommen *to come past*
Krankenhaus n *hospital*
Krankenpfleger m/f *nurse*
Kuchen m *cake*
Lehrer/Lehrerin m/f *teacher*
Leid n *pain*
    leiden *to suffer*
    das tut mir leid *I'm sorry*
    leider *unfortunately*
lieben *to love*
    lieb *dear*
    lieber *rather*
    ich trinke lieber Tee *I would prefer tea*
links *left*
los *let's go*
Lust *wish*
    haben Sie Lust? *do you want to?*
machen *to make*
    ich mache *I make*
    ich habe… gemacht *I have done/made it*
Mann m *("er)* *man, husband*
Messe f *trade fair*
Milch f *milk*
mit *with*
    mit/kommen *to come (with you)*
    mit/bringen *to bring (with you)*
mögen *to like*
    ich mag *I like*
    ich möchte *I would like*
morgen *tomorrow*
müde *tired*
nach *after/past*
    Nachmittag m *afternoon*
Nachspeise f *dessert*
nach *to*
    nach München *to Munich*
    nächste *next*
Nacht f *night*

nehmen *to take*
    ich nehme *I take*
nein *no*
nicht *not*
nie *never*
noch *still/yet/more*
nur *only*
oder *or*
ohne *without*
passen *to fit/suit*
    es passt mir gut *it fits me well*
Platz m *("e)* *place/square*
Postleitzahl f *postcode*
rechts *right*
reisen *to travel*
Reise f *journey*
Reisebüro n *travel agent*
Rückfahrkarte f *return ticket*
Schade! *pity! what a pity!*
schicken *to send*
Schloss n *castle*
Schlüssel m *key*
schnell *quick/fast*
schwimmen *to swim*
    ich schwimme *I swim*
schmecken *to taste*
sehen *to see*
    ich sehe *I see*
sehr *very*
sein *to be*
    ich bin *I am*
Seite f *(n)* *side or page*
sicher *surely definitely*
sie *she/they*
Sie *you (polite form)*
Skigebiet n *ski area*
spielen *to play*
sprechen *to speak*
steigen *to climb*
    einsteigen *to get on (transport)*
Straße f *(n)* *street*
    Straßenbahn f *the tram*
    Hauptstraße f *main street*

Stück *(n)*   *piece*
süß   *sweet*
teuer   *expensive*
treffen   *to meet*
trinken   *to drink*
trocken   *dry*
tschüs/tschüss/tschüssi   *bye*
Uhr f   *clock/hour*
um   *at/around*
    umsteigen   *to change (transport)*
    umziehen   *to change (clothes)*
verheiratet   *married*
verlobt   *engaged*
Verspätung f   *delay*
verstehen   *to understand*
viel/e   *many*
    vielen Dank   *many thanks*
Viertel   *quarter*
von   *of/from*
vor   *before*
    Vormittag   m *morning*

Vorwahlnummer f   *dialling code*
weiß   *white*
wissen   *to know*
    ich weiß   *I know*
weit   *far*
Woche f *(n)*   *week*
wohnen   *to live*
zahlen   *to pay*
Zeit f   *time*
ziehen   *to pull*
    durchziehen   *to pull through/ swipe a card*
ziemlich   *rather*
Zimmer n   *room*
zu   *to/too*
Zucker   m *sugar*
zuerst   *at first*
Zug m   *train*
    mit dem Zug   *by train*
Zuschlag   m *supplement*

English–German vocabulary

after   **nach**

(this) afternoon   **(heute) Nachmittag**

also   **auch**

always   **immer**

(I) am   **(ich) bin**

and   **und**

are   **sind**

big   **groß**

bigger   **größer**

brother   **der Bruder (¨)**

can you?   **kannst du?/können Sie?**

car   **das Auto (s)**

cheap   **billig**

   something cheaper   **etwas Billigeres**

child   **das Kind (er)**

colour   **die Farbe (n)**

daughter   **die Tochter (¨)**

day   **der Tag (e)**

difficult/hard   **schwer/schwierig**

divorced   **geschieden**

to do   **machen**

to drink   **trinken**

to eat   **essen**

engaged   **verlobt**

(this) evening   **(heute) Abend**

every day   **jeden Tag**

excuse me   **entschuldigen Sie, bitte**

expensive   **teuer**

far   **weit**

fast   **schnell**

for   **für**

I am looking forward to it   **ich freue mich darauf**

friend   **der Freund(e)/die Freundin(nen)**

in front of   **vor**

girl   **das Mädchen(¨)**

to go (on foot)   **gehen**; *to go (travel)*   **fahren**

good   **gut**

(he) has   **(er) hat,**

to have   **haben**

(I) have   **(ich) habe**; *have you…?*   **haben Sie …?**; *I haven't a …*   **ich habe kein/e/en…**

he   **er**

her   **ihr/e**

him   **ihn**

his   **sein/e**

how?   **wie?**; *how many?*   **wie viele?**

I   **ich**

in   **in**

is   **ist**

to live   **wohnen**

may I?   **darf ich?**

married   **verheiratet**

me   **mich**

Mr   **Herr**

Mrs   **Frau**

my   **mein/e**

new   **neu**

nice   **schön**

no   **nein**

old   **alt**

older   **älter**

pardon?   **wie bitte?**

parents   **die Eltern**

please   **bitte**

possible   **möglich**

quite   **ganz/ziemlich**

room   **das Zimmer**

she	**sie**	tomorrow	**morgen**
sister	**die Schwester (n)**	too	**zu**
short	**kurz**	I was	**ich war**
small	**klein**	week	**die Woche (n)**
smaller	**kleiner**	with	**mit**
son	**der Sohn(¨e)**	without	**ohne**
I'm sorry	**es tut mir Leid**	to work	**arbeiten**
thank you	**danke/vielen Dank**	I would like	**ich möchte**
their	**ihr/e**	yes	**ja**
there is/there are	**es gibt**	yesterday	**gestern**
they/them	**sie/sie**	young	**jung**
tired	**müde**	younger	**jünger**
to	**zu**	you	**Sie, du (ihr)**
today	**heute**		

Credits

Internal photos:

© Imagestate Media (John Foxx): page 23

© Karen Grigoryan – Fotolia: page 36

© Photodisc/Getty Images: pages 46, 74

© Imagestate Media: pages 88, 98, 110

© Ingram Publishing Limited: pages 12, 24, 66

© Steven Allan/iStockphoto.com: page 58